CULTURAL ATLAS FOR YOUNG PEOPLE

AFRICA

DR. JOCELYN MURRAY

UPDATED BY SEAN SHEEHAN

REVISED EDITION

Facts On File, Inc.

Cultural Atlas for Young People
AFRICA
Revised Edition

Published in North America by:
Facts On File, Inc.
132 West 31st Street
New York NY 10001

AN ANDROMEDA BOOK
Planned and produced by:
Andromeda Oxford Limited
11–13 The Vineyard, Abingdon
Oxfordshire OX14 3PX, United Kingdom
www.andromeda.co.uk

Publishing Director Graham Bateman
Project Manager Kim Richardson
Editor Lionel Bender
Art Director Ben White
Designer Malcolm Smythe
Cartographic Manager Richard Watts
Cartographic Editor Tim Williams
Picture Manager Claire Turner
Picture Researcher Cathy Statsny
Production Director Clive Sparling
Editorial and Administrative Assistants Marian Dreier,
   Rita Demetriou
Proofreader Lucy Poddington

ISBN: 0-8160-5151-8

Set ISBN: 0-8160-5144-5

Facts On File books are available at special discounts
when purchased in bulk quantities for businesses,
associations, institutions or sales promotions. Please
call our Special Sales Department in New York at
(212) 967-8800 or (800) 322-8755.

You can find Facts On File on the World Wide Web at
http://www.factsonfile.com

Originated in Hong Kong

Printed in Hong Kong by Paramount Ltd

10 9 8 7 6 5 4 3 2 1

This book is printed on acid-free paper.

Library of Congress Cataloging-in-Publication Data
available from Facts On File

Artwork and Picture Credits
Maps drawn by Lovell Johns, Oxford,
and Alan Mais, Hornchurch.

Key: t = top, b = bottom, c = center, l = left, r = right

Title page CF. 5 HL/Stephen Pern. 7 Clive Spong.
8 W. Kerremans. 8–9 WF. 10 HL/Patricio Goycolea.
12t SAL/C. Buxton. 12b Biofotos/H. Angel.
14 Dr Graham Speake, Oxford. 14–15 Richard and
Adam Hook. 16 Picturepoint, London. 17 WF. 18 Sonia
Halliday, Weston Turville, Bucks. 19t Roger Wood,
London. 19bl Elsevier Archives. 19br KM. 20bl WF.
20tr CF. 21 Elizabeth Photo Library, London.
22 Spectrum Colour Library, London. 22–23 KM.
24–25 KM. 25b W.H. Brooke/Fotomas Index, London.
26 RHPL/George Rainbird Ltd. 27 KM. 28l Sebastian
Münster. 28c,r Hulton Deutsch Collection, London.
29 KM 30tl HL. 30tr Father Kevin Carroll SMA, Cork,
Eire. 30bl WF. 30br Aspect Picture Library/Peter
Carmichael. 32–33 Chris Forsey. 33t Agence Hoa-Qui,
Paris. 34t Zefa Picture Library, London. 34c WF.
34b Aspect Picture Library/Larry Burrows. 35l RHPL.
35b Agence Hoa-Qui, Paris. 36 HL. 36–37 Gallo
Images/CORBIS. 37 WF. 38tl Royal Anthropological
Institute Photographic Collection, London. 38tc Klaus
Paysan, Stuttgart, Germany. 38tr Anne Cloudsley-
Thompson, London. 39t (left to right) Pitt Rivers
Museum, Oxford; Elizabeth Photo Library, London;
Pitt Rivers Museum, Oxford; Elizabeth Photo Library,
London. 39b Zefa Picture Library, London.
40t Dr H. Turner, Aberdeen. 40b HL/Sarah Errington.
41 CF. 42t Michael Holford, Loughton, Essex. 42c WF.

42b Dr H. Turner, Aberdeen. 43t WF. 43c Rex Lowden,
Stockport, England. 43b Richard and Adam Hook.
44 All photographs by Dr Gerhard Kubik, Vienna.
44–45 WF. 45t,c,b HL. 46–47 KM. 48–49 Chris
Forsey. 50 WF. 50–51 RHPL. 53 Sonia Halliday,
Weston Turville, Bucks. 54 CF. 54–55 HL. 55 KM.
56 Henri Stierlin, Geneva. 56–57 Chris Forsey.
57 RHPL/John G Ross. 60 WF. 60–61 KM. 62tl
Agence Hoa-Qui, Paris. 62tc HL. 62tr WF. 62–63 HL.
63t WF. 63b CF. 64t HL. 64b Magnum/Ian Berry.
65t HL/Sarah Errington. 65b HL. 66tc, bl Museum für
Völkerkünde, Vienna. 66–67 Bridgeman Art Library,
London. 67l Michael Holford, Loughton, Essex. 67r
Museum of Mankind, British Museum, London. 69l HL.
69c,b CF. 70–71 Richard and Adam Hook. 71br CF.
72 HL/A Singer. 74t HL. 74bl WF. 74br Agence
Hoa-Qui, Paris. 75tl Roger Wood, London. 75tr RHPL.
75b WF. 76 HL. 78t Aspect Picture Library, London.
78b CF. 79t KM. 79b HL. 80 Syndication International,
London. 82–83 KM. 83 Peter Garlake, London.
84t Agence Hoa-Qui, Paris. 84c Syndication
International, London. 84b A.A.A. Photo, Paris. 85tl CF.
85tr Zeta Picture Library, London. 85b De Beers Ltd,
London. 86 CF. 88t Aspect Picture Library, London.
88b A. Bannister. 89 KM. 90cl AH. 90tr Timothy
Beddow/HL. 90br CF.

List of Abbreviations
CF = Colorific!, London. HL = Hutchison Library,
London. KM = Kevin Maddison. RHPL = Robert
Harding Picture Library, London. SAL = Survival Anglia
Ltd, London. WF = Werner Forman Archive, London.

CONTENTS

INTRODUCTION

Most of Africa may have only been known to much of the rest of the Western world for just over 100 years. However, the continent has a rich and varied history and culture extending back many centuries before Europeans arrived. Indeed, the earliest human beings, as well as some of the first farmers in the world, seem to have all been Africans. And Arab travelers have visited Africa for nearly 1,000 years.

During the last 1,000 years of African history, a number of great empires and kingdoms have risen, prospered, and fallen. Some of these were in many ways more advanced than the European states of the time. These empires and kingdoms are remembered today in the names of modern African countries such as Mali, Benin, and Zimbabwe.

Climate and geography have significantly shaped African history and culture. Even today, in many regions, these factors are a hindrance and barrier to the free movement of people. But they did not prevent Europeans from coming to Africa from the 15th century onwards to trade with its states, enslave many millions of its peoples and explore and colonize its lands.

Like Europe and Asia, Africa has many languages and peoples but, unlike these other continents, African languages were spoken and not written until quite recently. There were no records of the past written in native languages. How then do we know of Africa's past? Our knowledge has come from four main sources. Firstly, Arab writers and travelers visited the East coast and the lands of West Africa from the 10th century onwards. Their written accounts, often of daily life as well as of great events, have provided valuable information. Secondly, tracing the movement of languages provides an important clue when trying to follow developments in the history of ancient Africa. Thirdly, archeological evidence has been used to piece together African history. The final source of information is the oral (spoken) history of Africans themselves – tales of past events handed down from generation to generation over many centuries.

Art, architecture, and music also help in the understanding of the cultural history, and in this book you will find articles devoted to these subjects as well as to the history of the African continent.

Africa is divided into two main sections. The first, **The History of Africa**, builds up the story of the continent from prehistoric times, through the Ancient Greek and Roman periods followed by Arab and European invasions, to the emergence of all present-day African cultures and societies. Throughout this section there are maps illustrating specific themes or topics in the main text. Many of these are accompanied by charts giving important dates and events in African history. The second part, **A Regional Guide to Africa**, looks at the countries and peoples of modern Africa. It includes typical atlas-style maps containing details of towns, cities, rivers, railroads, and country borders. These are accompanied by charts giving key dates in African history since the end of the Second World War in 1945. Important African towns can be located on these maps using the Gazetteer on page 93.

Our survey of Africa is arranged in double-page spreads. Each spread is a complete story. So you can either read the book from beginning to end, or just dip into it to learn about a specific topic. A Glossary on page 92 explains important historical and African terms used in the book.

Abbreviations used in this book
BCE = Before Common Era (also known as BC).
CE = Common Era (also known as AD). c. = circa (about). in = inch. yd = yard. ft = foot. mi = mile.

Right In Mali, a Dogon villager wears a mask and chestplate covered with cowrie shells as a sign of wealth.

TABLE OF DATES

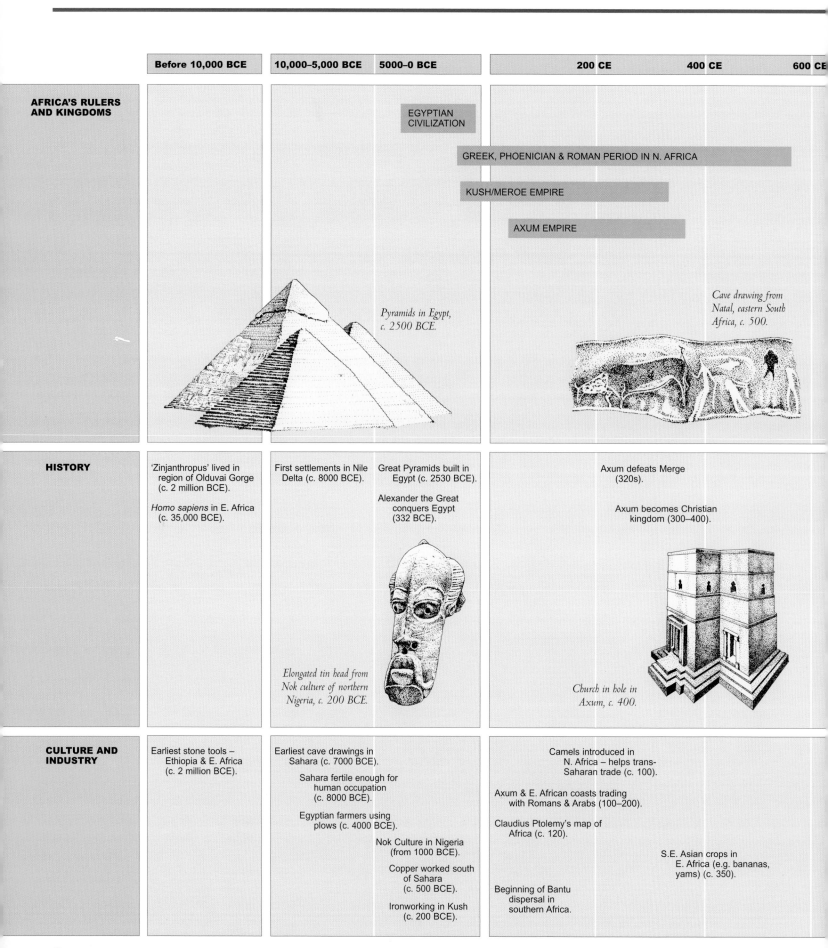

	Before 10,000 BCE	10,000–5,000 BCE	5000–0 BCE	200 CE	400 CE	600 CE
AFRICA'S RULERS AND KINGDOMS			EGYPTIAN CIVILIZATION			
				GREEK, PHOENICIAN & ROMAN PERIOD IN N. AFRICA		
				KUSH/MEROE EMPIRE		
				AXUM EMPIRE		

Pyramids in Egypt, c. 2500 BCE.

Cave drawing from Natal, eastern South Africa, c. 500.

| **HISTORY** | 'Zinjanthropus' lived in region of Olduvai Gorge (c. 2 million BCE). *Homo sapiens* in E. Africa (c. 35,000 BCE). | First settlements in Nile Delta (c. 8000 BCE). | Great Pyramids built in Egypt (c. 2530 BCE). Alexander the Great conquers Egypt (332 BCE). | Axum defeats Merge (320s). Axum becomes Christian kingdom (300–400). | | |

Elongated tin head from Nok culture of northern Nigeria, c. 200 BCE.

Church in hole in Axum, c. 400.

| **CULTURE AND INDUSTRY** | Earliest stone tools – Ethiopia & E. Africa (c. 2 million BCE). | Earliest cave drawings in Sahara (c. 7000 BCE). Sahara fertile enough for human occupation (c. 8000 BCE). Egyptian farmers using plows (c. 4000 BCE). | Nok Culture in Nigeria (from 1000 BCE). Copper worked south of Sahara (c. 500 BCE). Ironworking in Kush (c. 200 BCE). | Camels introduced in N. Africa – helps trans-Saharan trade (c. 100). Axum & E. African coasts trading with Romans & Arabs (100–200). Claudius Ptolemy's map of Africa (c. 120). Beginning of Bantu dispersal in southern Africa. | S.E. Asian crops in E. Africa (e.g. bananas, yams) (c. 350). | |

KANEM & BORNO EMPIRES

PORTUGUESE RULE IN E. AFRICA

BENIN EMPIRE IN W. AFRICA

COLONIAL PERIOD
rule by British, French, Spanish, Portuguese, Belgians, Germans, Italians, Dutch, Turks,

GHANA EMPIRE IN W. SUDAN

MALI EMPIRE IN W. AFRICA

ERA OF TRANS-ATLANTIC SLAVE TRADE

TAKRUR EMPIRE IN W. AFRICA

SONGHAY EMPIRE

OYO & ASANTE EMPIRES

SHONA EMPIRE & EMPIRE OF MONOMOTAPAS (ZIMBABWE)

MUSLIM RULE IN E., W., & N. AFRICA

Great Zimbabwe, a large stone-walled enclosure built by the Shona people c.1200–1400.

Fort Jesus at Mombasa, Kenya, built by the Portuguese 1593–96.

The countries of Africa became independent in the 20th century and are now ruled by African leaders.

Axum (Ethiopia) threatened by Muslims; Isolated from Christian Europe (600–700).

Egypt conquered by Arabs (646).

Carthage conquered by Muslim Arabs (695).

Great Age of Islam in N. Africa begun (800–900).

Muslim 'Almoravids' invade Ghana (1087).

Ghana defeated by Sundiata of Mali (1240).

Reign of Mansa Musa in Mali (1307–37); his pilgrimage to Mecca (1324–25).

Portuguese in Kongo (1482).

Vasco Da Gama round Cape Good Hope (1498).

Portugal established E. Coast forts (from 1509).

Turks occupy Egypt (1517).

Hausa States in Nigeria (Kano/Katsina) (1510–40).

Moroccan invasion of Songhay (1591).

Osei Tutu creates Asante Union (1697).

First contact between Boers & Bantu (1778).

Napoleonic Wars: Battles of the Nile & Alexandria (1798 & 1801).

Fulani Empire in W. Africa (1800–1900).

Congo Free State established by Belgium (1884).

Boer War in S. Africa (1898–1902).

Mau-Mau movement in Kenya (1952–60).

Ghana independent (1957).

French West African Colonies independent (1960).

Portuguese colonies independent (1975).

Zimbabwe independent (1979).

Compound of houses on steep hillsides built by Dogon people in Mali from about 1500.

Trans-Saharan trade expands (from c. 800).

Use of iron widespread in Africa (c. 650).

E. Africa part of Indian Ocean trade area – visited by Arabs & Chinese (c. 800).

Islam established south of Sahara (c. 1000).

Slaves exported to N. Africa from Guinea (c. 1150).

Early buildings at Great Zimbabwe (c. 1200).

Yoruba sculptures at Ife (from 1250).

Ibn Battuta visits Mali (1352).

University at Timbuktu (c. 1450).

Asante exports gold north (c. 1550–1650).

Portuguese introduce S. American crops (e.g. cassava, maize) to Africa (c. 1500).

British ban on slave-trading (1807).

Opening of Suez Canal (1869).

Discovery of diamonds in S. Africa (1874).

First major railway systems built in E. and S. Africa (1880–1900).

African porter carrying ivory tusk for Europeans "on safari," c. 1850.

PART ONE

THE HISTORY OF AFRICA

Above *A carved and polished wooden mask used by the Chokwe people of the Democratic Republic of Congo in religious ceremonies.*

Right *Pillars of dried mud in front of the mosque at Jenne, in Mali, West Africa. The mosque was built of dried mud on a wooden framework.*

GEOGRAPHY OF AFRICA

AFRICA, THE SECOND LARGEST CONTINENT (after Asia), is well over three times larger than the United States. Its greatest north–south length is 5,000mi, its greatest width 4,650mi. The equator lies almost across its center, but two-thirds of its area is in the northern hemisphere. Although three-quarters of Africa lies within the tropics, the climate is affected more by altitude, or land height, and distance from the sea (see pages 12–13).

FORMATION OF THE AFRICAN LANDMASS

Africa once lay at the heart of a supercontinent called Pangea. About 180 million years ago the separate parts of this great united continent began to drift apart. The African and Asian parts are divided only by the narrow Red Sea, but the whole Atlantic Ocean separates them from the American parts. The continents are still slowly drifting. In Africa comparatively recent movement has left weak strips, called fault lines. These make up one of the longest "rift systems" in the world (see small map).

At the extreme northwest and southeast of Africa are young mountain ranges. But most of the continent consists of vast flat lands or plateaus (tablelands) at different levels. Where the plateaus have many rivers and streams, a large lake sometimes forms at the lowest level – like Lake Chad. Around the edges of the plateaus, along the coasts, are narrow plains.

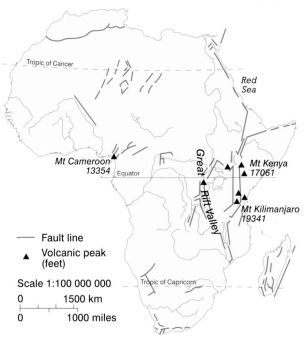

Fault line

▲ Volcanic peak (feet)

Scale 1:100 000 000

0   1500 km

0   1000 miles

Mt Cameroon 13354

Mt Kenya 17061

Mt Kilimanjaro 19341

Great Rift Valley

Tropic of Cancer

Red Sea

Equator

Tropic of Capricorn

Madeira Islands (PORTUGAL)

Canary Islands (SPAIN)

WESTERN SAHARA (MOROCCO)

MAURITANIA
■ Nouakchott

Dakar ■   **SENEGAL**

Banjul ■   Gambia

GAMBIA

Bissau ■   Fouta Djallon   Bamak

GUINEA-BISSAU   **GUINEA**

Conakry ■

Freetown ■

SIERRA LEONE

Monrovia ■

LIBERIA

Senegal

Above In geology, a rift is a steep-sided valley formed as a section of the Earth's crust sinks between two or more fault lines. The African Rift system runs from the Red Sea into Malawi and Mozambique. Its best-known section is Kenya's Great Rift Valley.

Right Africa's coastlines are regular, with few inlets to provide good deepwater harbors. Apart from Madagascar, islands are small and few.

For a large continent, Africa has few great rivers, and those that exist often have rapids and waterfalls where they pass over the edges of steep plateaus. Where the land is flatter, rivers are often winding. Rivers have therefore been of little use for long-distance transport. Like the lakes, they have been useful only for fairly local movement.

Left Looking down from the Eastern Rift in Kenya. In East Africa, there are two main branches of the Great Rift Valley: eastern and western. The Eastern Rift runs past Mt Kenya and Mt Kilimanjaro, which are extinct volcanoes, and in places its walls fall 2,600ft from the plateaus on either side of it.

CLIMATE AND VEGETATION

Rainfall in Africa mainly occurs in particular seasons, but it is unpredictable and varies greatly from region to region. Some years there is enough rain for farming, in others there is none and droughts occur.

At Africa's extreme north and south the climate is like that in Mediterranean Europe, with distinct seasons. Along the north coast there are wet winters in December and January. In South Africa winter is in July and August.

In the hot deserts of North Africa, northeast Africa and southwest Africa, there is little rain at any time of the year. The tropical rainforests, in West Africa and west central Africa, are always hot and wet: rain falls most months.

ON PLATEAUS AND MOUNTAINS

Over the rest of the continent, temperature is largely affected by altitude of the land and distance from the sea, rather than by latitude. This is why Africa is drier and less hot than you might expect. There are dry, cold periods but no true winters.

North of the equator July is the hottest, driest month. In the south January is hottest. The rains in the northern hemisphere fall around March–April ("the long rains") and October ("the short rains").

During the rainy season, the rain usually falls very hard. In a typical day there will be heavy rain from nightfall to the early morning, followed by a clear, and even sunny, day. (Near the equator night and day are of roughly equal length.) Thunderstorms are frequent, especially in the tropics and around the great lakes (Chad, Victoria, Malawi).

On the plateaus, vegetation varies from forests to grassy plains and drier, rough-grass plains (savanna or "veldt") with acacia and bottle-shaped baobab trees. In the mountain regions bands of bamboo, heather, lichens, and alpine plants occur.

CHANGES IN VEGETATION

The vegetation of Africa was once quite different. In Roman times, large areas of North Africa were fertile grain-growing regions and tropical rainforests spread right across central Africa. But, mainly as a result of poor farming methods and the cutting down of trees, desert and scrubland increased and forest decreased.

Left South of the dry northern deserts, inland Africa, except for the mountains and rainforests, is dry savanna, with short grasses and thorn-trees (acacia). This is perfect country for large animals such as zebras, giraffes, and elephants. Where elephants become too numerous, they can damage the vegetation, as here in Tanzania.

Below High up on Mt Elgon in western Kenya the vegetation is more alpine than tropical. Plants related to the ragworts of wastelands in temperate regions have evolved these stumpy forms.

Below and right *The type of vegetation (right) that grows depends on rainfall (below), temperature (bottom), and type of soil. Where there is little or no rain, plants cannot grow,* *as in the great deserts of North Africa. In the plateaus and mountains differences between day and night temperatures are often much greater than between seasons.*

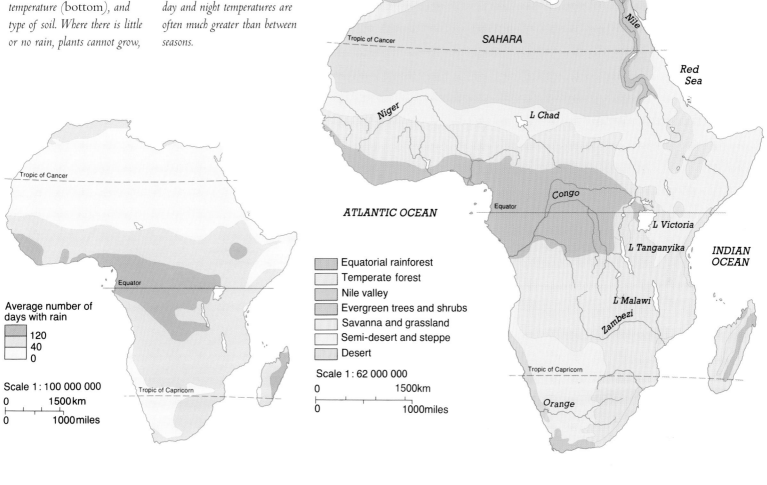

Mediterranean Sea

Tropic of Cancer

SAHARA

Nile

Red Sea

Niger

L Chad

ATLANTIC OCEAN

Congo

Equator

L Victoria

L Tanganyika

INDIAN OCEAN

L Malawi

Zambezi

Tropic of Capricorn

Orange

Equatorial rainforest
Temperate forest
Nile valley
Evergreen trees and shrubs
Savanna and grassland
Semi-desert and steppe
Desert

Scale 1 : 62 000 000

0   1500km

0   1000miles

Tropic of Cancer

Equator

Average number of days with rain

120
40
0

Scale 1 : 100 000 000

0   1500km

0   1000miles

Tropic of Capricorn

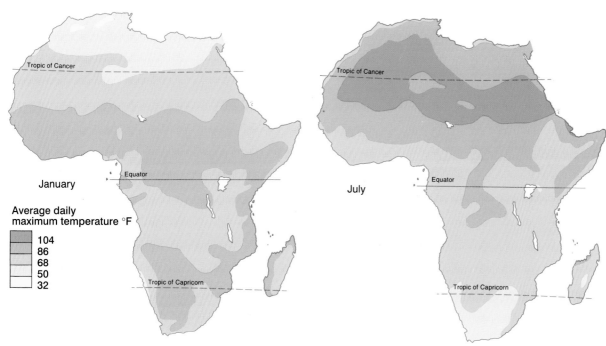

Tropic of Cancer

Equator

January

Average daily maximum temperature °F

104
86
68
50
32

Tropic of Capricorn

Tropic of Cancer

Equator

July

Tropic of Capricorn

Left *These two temperature maps show that north of the equator it is hotter in July than it is in January, but in the south it is the opposite. Throughout Africa, perhaps more than anywhere else in the world, the vegetation and climate greatly influence the wealth and variety of wildlife and peoples' way of life — whether people are farmers or hunter-gatherers, the type of houses they build and their customs, beliefs, art, and music.*

THE EARLIEST HUMANS

RESEARCH OF PLACES IN EASTERN AND southern Africa where fossils have been found has led us to accept Charles Darwin's claim, 150 years ago, that Africa must have been the home of the earliest human beings. The most famous site is Olduvai Gorge, northern Tanzania. Using fossils from this and other sites, a story of human development unfolds, stretching from 1 million to 5 million years ago.

RELATED TO MONKEYS?

It is no longer claimed that humans are descended from monkeys. Instead it is recognized that human beings and the apes (gibbons, chimpanzees, gorillas, orangutans) have a common ancestor. They are distantly related – as some kind of cousins. Several million years ago members of a species of ape-like creatures developed in two different ways. One continued to use all four limbs for walking; the other stood erect on two legs, leaving two limbs free for carrying and, eventually, tool-using. We evolved from this second group. A new find in Chad in 2002 suggests that the earliest known members of this group lived 7 million years ago.

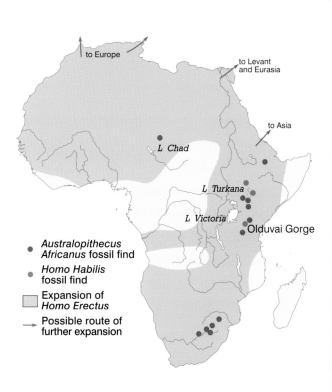

Sites of the Early and Middle Stone Age

Fossils of Homo habilis (tool-using humans) in association with pebble tools, have been found at sites near Lake Turkana in northern Kenya and at Olduvai Gorge. They have been dated to between 1 and 2½ million years ago. Fossils of Homo erectus (upright humans), with hand axes, have been found widely, and are dated from 100,000 to 1 million years ago. The sites marked are those where excavations since 1950 have been made. The Middle Stone Age marks more varied developments in lifestyle over different parts of Africa.

to Europe
to Levant and Eurasia
to Asia
L Chad
L Turkana
L Victoria
Olduvai Gorge

● *Australopithecus Africanus* fossil find
● *Homo Habilis* fossil find
▢ Expansion of *Homo Erectus*
→ Possible route of further expansion

Above *Masked hunters attack eland in this scene from a rock shelter painting in KwaZulu-Natal, South Africa. Cave paintings, found widely south of the Sahara, are often linked with earlier hunter-gatherer peoples like the San of present-day southern Africa.*

Right Homo habilis *men chip away at rocks, sharpening them for cutting up game or scraping hides. The game would be trapped in a pit or run down by several men. A woman, with her child, gathers wild berries. Branches were collected to make shelters.*

14

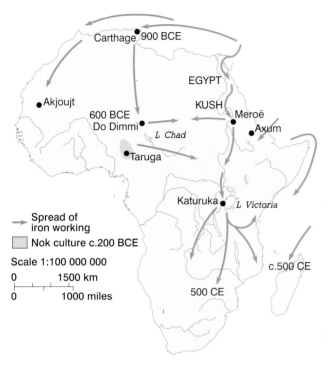

Bantu culture

Bantu, meaning "the people," is the name given to a group of closely related languages spoken in southern Africa. Archeological evidence suggests a common culture spreading southward between 500 BCE and 1000 CE, and this is associated with a movement of Bantu-speakers from the north.

The culture shares similarities in pottery, agriculture, and the use of ironworking. The Bantu migration may have helped spread ironworking skills into central and southern Africa, starting around 200 BCE. By 500 CE, Bantu culture was common in these areas.

Skulls of the two-footed ape-like animal, *Australopithecus africanus*, have been found in eastern and southern Africa. From this stock came *Homo habilis*, the first toolmaker and so-called hominid, from whom *Homo erectus*, "upright human," and "modern (or wise) human," *Homo sapiens*, are descended.

THE STONE AGE AND EARLY IRON AGE

Many shaped and sharpened pebbles used by *Homo habilis* have been found. Their remains have been discovered in Kenya, Uganda, Tanzania, and Ethiopia. Many thousands of years later in hominid development (Middle Stone Age) came hand axes, with a sharp stone fixed to a handle. At this time (I million years ago), speech was probably developing, allowing the passing on of the toolmaker's craft.

During the Late Stone Age, about 20,000 years ago, when *Homo erectus* was moving into Europe and Asia, smaller and more exact tools such as bows and arrows were invented.

The Iron Age began in the Middle East around 1200 BCE. It spread to the coast of North Africa, and then to West Africa along ancient trade routes.

THE KINGDOMS OF AFRICA

FROM THE EARLIEST TIMES, PEOPLE HAVE lived together to provide for their needs – food, clothing, shelter, and defense. The family – parents and children – is the smallest unit. Several related families together make up a clan, or tribe. In some parts of Africa people lived with no more organization than this. The Kikuyu of Kenya and Igbo of Nigeria are successful examples of tribes with village governments in which the "elders" acted as judges or leaders. More usually people joined together in a larger "state" with a strong, central leader like a chief or king.

EARLY KINGDOMS

Ancient Egypt, which flourished as a civilization as long as 4,500 years ago, was the first of these states. Farther south along the Nile another kingdom, Kush, emerged around 700 BCE and later grew around the town of Meroë.

Some early kingdoms began when outsiders tried to conquer local clans, who then joined together for defense. In North Africa, when Phoenician traders from the region of present-day Syria founded the city of Carthage, groups united against them formed in Numidia (now Algeria) and in Mauretania (Morocco). Later, when Muslim Arabs came to North Africa from the east, kingdoms were founded, both by them and by the local peoples who were defending themselves against the Muslim armies.

Where there was active trading, local leaders organized the collection of taxes and duties. They became rich, gained power, and often made themselves kings. In West Africa, where there was

Right This map shows that there were kingdoms in much of Africa, although not all of them existed at the same time. Almost all were of African origin; only along the northern coastline and in the East African city-states were outsiders the founders. The process of powerful rulers building kingdoms continued right up to the early 19th century, when it was largely stopped by European conquest.

Left Kings of the early kingdom of Axum on the Red Sea set up tall stones, some over 100ft high, called monoliths or stelae above the royal tombs. Once there were more than a hundred, now only this one remains standing.

By about 1 CE Axum, controlling Red Sea trade through the port of Adulis, had become a rich and powerful state, from which the inland kingdom of Ethiopia was later to develop. Through the port there were trading connections with Greece, Arabia, and India.

In the 4th century the king of Axum adopted Christianity, but by the 6th century came under the influence of growing Islamic power.

Mediterranean Sea

Carthage

NUMIDIA

Tripoli

MAURETANIA

TRIPOLITANIA   CYRENAICA   Cairo

Nile

EGYPT

Red
Sea

MALI   KUSH

TAKRUR

GHANA   SONGHAY

Senegal   Niger   DARFUR   Meroë   Adulis

Katsina   L Chad   AXUM

Segou   BORNO   KANEM   ETHIOPIA

Kano

Oyo   HAUSA

ASANTE   YORUBA   BENIN

DAHOMEY   IGBO

BUNYORO

Congo   Mogadishu

ATLANTIC OCEAN   BUGANDA

ANKOLE   L Victoria   Malindi

LOBA   RWANDA   Mombasa

BURUNDI   Zanzibar

LUNDA

Kilwa

MBUNDU   BEMBA

Zambezi

Great Zimbabwe

SHONA   Sofala

BUGANDA   Major African kingdom

•   Pre-colonial town

Scale 1 : 62 000 000

0   1500km

0   1000miles

TSWANA

Orange   SWAZI

ZULU

LESOTHO   INDIAN OCEAN

gold and great markets, traders went across the Sahara desert as far as Egypt with metals, salt, cloth, and ivory. Yoruba and Igbo people, who dyed cloth and made leather and metal goods, formed many small kingdoms. Ghana, and later Mali, Songhay, and Kanem-Borno, were powerful, well-organized kingdoms according to the Muslim travelers and writers who visited them. Islam, the Muslim religion, became well established among the ruling families of all these empires.

MIGRATION, TRADE, AND CITY-STATES

In central Africa, kingdoms were established as the Bantu-speaking peoples began moving east across the region, introducing new crops suited to the climate (bananas, yams, millet). This caused a rapid growth in population in the Congo forests. The kingdoms of Kongo and Ngola were powerful rivals when the Portuguese arrived here in the late 1400s.

Along the coast of East Africa, Arab traders had settled over many centuries. These Muslim outsiders became wealthy from trade with Asia across the Indian Ocean, and founded a number of city-states or kingdoms in which they were the rulers of the local people. One of the most powerful was the kingdom of Axum, which controlled parts of southern Arabia.

Below The entrance to a group of dwellings in Kano city. The walls are made of sun-baked mud. Kano was one of the earliest, and in the 16th century one of the largest, city-states of the Hausa kingdom, Nigeria.

Major African kingdoms, 3000 BCE–1850 CE

From 3000 BCE Egypt united under the pharaohs.
8th century BCE Phoenicians found Carthage, trading center of their many colonies.
1st century CE Kingdom of Axum flourishing.
7th century Arab conquests along North African coast. Carthage destroyed in 697.
8th to 9th centuries Kingdoms of Borno and Kanem flourish to west and east of Lake Chad.
13th to 15th centuries Rise of Ethiopia, Kingdom of Mali, Great Zimbabwe.
From 15th century Rise of Bantu states in Congo (Democratic Republic of Congo) and around the great East African lakes.
18th century Kingdoms of Benin (Nigeria) and also Asante (Ghana) flourishing.
Early 19th century Chaka Zulu conquering peoples of southern Africa.
19th century Moshoeshoe establishes Lesotho kingdom.

GREEKS AND ROMANS IN AFRICA

THE MEDITERRANEAN IS ALMOST AN inland sea. It has been well traveled for thousands of years. So it is not very surprising that the peoples who lived on its northern, eastern, and western shores – Romans, Greeks, and Phoenicians – became interested in the lands to the south.

EGYPT UNDER GREECE AND ROME

The Greeks had for long traded with Egypt, and in the 4th century BCE King Alexander the Great of Macedonia (now part of Greece, Macedon, and Bulgaria), conquered it. In 331 he founded the city called after him. Alexandria, near modern Cairo, became a very great and important center of Greek culture and influence.

After Alexander's death, his empire was divided. One of his generals, Ptolemy, made himself king of Egypt, and after him all Egyptian kings were called Ptolemy. Ptolemy I's kingdom was the longest-lasting of the empire.

By the 2nd century BCE the Romans, too, were interested in Egypt, as they were extending their power all around the Mediterranean. In 51 BCE a brother and sister, Ptolemy XIII and the more famous Cleopatra VII, ruled Egypt together, but by 30 BCE the Emperor Augustus had made Egypt a Roman province.

CARTHAGE AND ROMAN AFRICA

Carthage had been founded by Phoenician traders, and by the 3rd century BCE the Carthaginians were powerful enough to fight against Roman expansion. After three long series of battles by land and sea, in the end, in 146 BCE, the Carthaginians were defeated. Rome sacked Carthage and took over the province it named Africa. The city was rebuilt as a Roman city, but the original people kept their own language and some of their customs. Later, Carthage (like Alexandria before) was to become a very important Christian center, in the days before Islam came from Arabia.

Right The amphitheater at El Djem (south of Carthage) was one of the largest in the Roman Empire. It was built in the 3rd century CE to replace an earlier one. As at Rome, gladiators fought and chariots raced to amuse the people.

Below Long before the Romans came to North Africa, Dougga was a prosperous city. It held a strong defensive position 55mi southwest of Carthage. The Libyan and Punic inhabitants lived alongside the Roman citizens, who built their own amenities, like this temple of the gods Jupiter, Juno, and Minerva.

Cyrenaica, 500mi to the west of Alexandria, became a Roman province in 74 BCE, together with the island of Crete. It had previously been made a place of Greek settlement by Ptolemy I. The chief city of Cyrenaica was Cyrene. To its west lay another great Roman province, Numidia, "nomads" land.

The semi-nomadic Berbers who lived in the Sahara desert on the fringes of these two Roman provinces were almost certainly the contacts or go-betweens used by the Romans to trade with the black peoples living to the south of the desert. Rock drawings 2,000 years old and depicting horse-drawn vehicles, prove the existence of trade routes between the coast and the interior of Africa.

The Greek and Roman empires in Africa

330 BCE Alexander the Great of Macedonia conquers Egypt. City of Alexandria founded.
246–241 BCE, 221–183 BCE First and second (Punic) wars between Rome and Carthage.
218 BCE Hannibal of Carthage marches across Alps to Italy and defeats Romans in battle.
146 BCE Third war between Rome and Carthage. Carthage lost. Rome takes over Province of Africa.
74 BCE Cyrenaica becomes a Roman province.
47 BCE Cleopatra VII queen in Egypt.
44 BCE Death of Julius Caesar.
31 BCE Mark Antony and Cleopatra defeated by Octavian (Emperor Augustus). Egypt now ruled from Rome.
40 CE Mauretania becomes a Roman province.

Right Slaves load ivory into the hold of a Roman boat.

Below There was a great deal of trade between North Africa and the Greeks. Later, the Roman Empire depended on Egyptian corn. Other exports were papyrus, flax, olives, dates, wine, and rare animals. This map, published in 1630, names those parts of Europe, Asia, and Africa forming the Greek Empire of the 2nd century BCE.

EUROPEANS IN AFRICA

FOR A VERY LONG TIME, AFRICA WAS AN unknown continent to the people of Europe. Even its shape was like a great question mark. Only the northern coasts, around the south of the Mediterranean, were familiar to Europeans until about 600 years ago.

Claudius Ptolemy, who lived in Alexandria in the 2nd century CE, published a map of Africa. It was not a good map, but for hundreds of years there was nothing better. The Arabs, who had explored the north and east coasts, knew most about Africa. Ibn Battuta, a Moroccan Berber who lived in the 14th century, wrote of his journeys to Egypt, East and West Africa (as well as to India and China).

EUROPEAN EXPLOITATION BEGINS

In the 15th century, when the Portuguese began looking for a sea route to the East, more information came. In 1497 Vasco da Gama set sail

Right Open-air markets, such as this one in Luxor, Egypt, have for centuries been the great trading places of Africa. Here a tailor works at his sewing machine, producing traditional garments with modern methods.

Below African artists have often used traditional styles to comment on their new colonial situation. Here, a woodworker from the Democratic Republic of Congo has carved the Belgian official of the 1920s in his chauffeur-driven car.

Colonial development from the 1870s

From 1876 to 1884 there occurred an unofficial scramble among the European nations for regions of Africa that had great mineral resources — gold, diamonds, copper — and potentially fertile farmland. By 1895 all but the Sahara region had been shared out between seven of them as some 50 separate kingdoms, states, or countries. Subsequently, the colonial boundaries

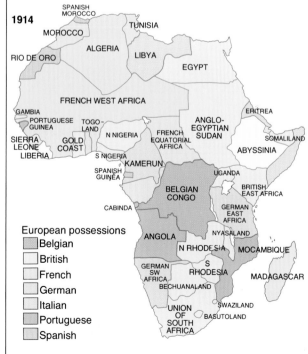

1914

SPANISH MOROCCO
MOROCCO
TUNISIA
RIO DE ORO
ALGERIA
LIBYA
EGYPT
FRENCH WEST AFRICA
GAMBIA
PORTUGUESE GUINEA
TOGO-LAND
N NIGERIA
FRENCH EQUATORIAL AFRICA
ANGLO-EGYPTIAN SUDAN
ERITREA
SOMALILAND
SIERRA LEONE
LIBERIA
GOLD COAST
S NIGERIA
KAMERUN
ABYSSINIA
SPANISH GUINEA
UGANDA
BRITISH EAST AFRICA
BELGIAN CONGO
GERMAN EAST AFRICA
CABINDA
ANGOLA
NYASALAND
N RHODESIA
MOCAMBIQUE
GERMAN SW AFRICA
S RHODESIA
MADAGASCAR
BECHUANALAND
SWAZILAND
UNION OF SOUTH AFRICA
BASUTOLAND

European possessions
- Belgian
- British
- French
- German
- Italian
- Portuguese
- Spanish

from Portugal to Calicut, in India, traveling around the coasts of Africa (see page 22). His ship rested in harbors along the way, and here he put up stone crosses that may still be seen today.

Portuguese traders and missionaries soon followed. In West Africa, English, French, Dutch, and Swedish traders joined the Portuguese. They exchanged European goods for African products, at first gold and ivory, but by the 18th century the most popular "product" came to be slaves (see pages 24–25). The port-cities at the European end (Liverpool, Bristol, Nantes, Lisbon, Bordeaux, and others) grew wealthy from this barbarous trade.

SETTLERS AND EXPLORERS

In the mid-17th century Dutch farmers were sent to the Cape of Good Hope as employees of the Dutch East India Company to grow food for crews of the Dutch ships that passed on the long journey to Indonesia. After a few years some of the Dutch who wanted to keep cattle moved farther inland from Cape Town. They had in fact become settlers.

By 1800 Europeans knew a good deal about the coasts of Africa but they knew very little about the land beyond them. The 19th century was the age of European exploration of the interior, and before the end of the century most of Africa had come under European rule.

The nations that acquired most colonies were Great Britain, France, Portugal, and Germany (until the First World War). Spain, Belgium, and The Netherlands also ruled some areas, and later Italy. Liberia (which had strong connections with the United States) and Ethiopia (until it was conquered by Italy in the late 1930s) stayed independent.

THE END OF THE COLONIAL PERIOD

The colonial period lasted only about 80 years. The end of the Second World War in 1945 saw a decline in the power of Britain, Germany, and France. Nationalism saw a new wave of countries begin to assert their sense of separate identity. The result was that African colonies began to gain their independence, the first being the Gold Coast (Ghana) in 1957. Most kept some connection with the European country that had once ruled over them, for example using its language as their own international language, trading with it, and receiving some development aid from it.

continually changed with the bargains made between European powers. More than 80 years of colonial rule saw the foundations laid for modern Africa's communications (especially railways), education system and civil administration. Africans educated and trained by Europeans became the leaders of the independent African nations.

Above View of Beni Abbes, a small Algerian town. The small dome in the center is the mosque, a visible symbol of Islam. On the hill is the former French fort, recalling the days of colonialism and the French Foreign Legion. Trees and palms shelter and fringe the town.

THE PORTUGUESE

THE PORTUGUESE SAILED SOUTH ALONG West Africa from 1415 and rounded the Cape of Good Hope in 1497. Vasco da Gama took the route to India in 1497, and on his first sea journey called at Mombasa, Malindi, and other East African ports (1498). From then until the fall of Fort Jesus at Mombasa in 1698, Portugal was the leading east coast power, from Mogadishu in Somalia to Sofala in Mozambique. For nearly 300 years, until 1975, Mozambique remained their trading base.

What did the Portuguese want? First, places where their ships could rest and refit on the long journey to India, and take on food and water. Second, profitable trade. The traders lived in coastal settlements where African rulers gave them permission to build stores and forts. At Mombasa on the east coast they built Fort Jesus as a stronghold against the Arabs. Third, a region where their Catholic missionaries could fulfill their duties of religious conversion. In Africa there were pagan Africans, Muslims and, in Ethiopia, Christians who did not belong to the Roman Catholic Church.

CONQUERORS AND MISSIONARIES

The east coast city-states were already part of a trading network controlled by Omani Arabs. Goods came from the Middle East, India, and even from China. To profit from this trade, the Portuguese had to control the cities.

After da Gama's second voyage to India (1502), they began to capture territories by force. In 1505 they occupied Sofala, and in 1506 set up a military base at Kilwa and pillaged Mombasa. These and other cities were taken with much violence and cruelty. But the number of Portuguese officials and soldiers was never more than a few thousand and there were several revolts against their rule. Muslims were defending not only their religion but also the Arab control of the Indian Ocean network of trade.

Roman Catholic missionaries had initially had some success in parts of southern Africa (in Angola-Congo in 1518 an African had been made bishop). But few Africans were converted to Christianity in the strongly Islamic cultures of the East African cities. Those who did convert were persecuted by the Muslims.

In 1614, Yusuf, Mombasa's young sultan, was taken to Goa in Portuguese India for education. In 1630 he returned a Christian with a Portuguese wife, but in 1631 led a revolt against the Portuguese during which Christians were killed. He died a Muslim in 1637.

Perhaps the most important contribution of the Portuguese in Africa was the introduction of new foods, mainly from Brazil: cassava (manioc) and maize, and fruit and nut trees like guava, avocado pears, and cashew.

Below The Portuguese built Fort Jesus in 1592–95 with the help of workmen from India. Even this stronghold did not protect them — after a siege of nearly three years, it was taken by the Omani Arabs in 1698.

Right On the busy quayside of an East African port, Portuguese and Omani traders haggle over goods unloaded from dhows. The Portuguese needed cloth, beads, porcelain, and metal tools and implements for their trade with African chiefs. Some of these they brought from Portugal; other goods were obtained from Omani Arab traders, or direct from India.

They traded these goods for gold, which came through Sofala in the south, other metals, ivory, and later slaves (most of whom went to Brazil). They also played a part in local trade up and down the coast, mostly for foods of various kinds and pottery. In the ruins of almost all the old coastal cities plates and coins from China, brought by Arab ships, have been found.

THE AFRICAN SLAVE TRADE

WHEN EUROPEAN TRADERS FIRST BEGAN buying from Africans, they wanted gold and other metals, and ivory. But they soon found that it was even more profitable to buy and sell African people – that is, slaves. In the Americas and the West Indies workers were needed for the tobacco, cotton, and sugar plantations. African rulers were willing to sell Africans captured from neighboring territories in order to obtain European goods, especially firearms. African states without rifles and ammunition were vulnerable to their neighbors. And so a terrible trade in human beings began.

TRADING IN HUMAN MISERY

Slave traders from Spain, Portugal, and Great Britain began sending slave ships to West and central Africa in the 16th century. The trade reached its peak in the mid-18th century. Probably more than 12 million men, women, and children were taken from Africa. Arabs in East Africa also bought slaves, whom they sold in the Middle East and India, and the Portuguese also sold some to Brazil. But the numbers of slaves taken from East Africa were far fewer as at the time this part of the continent was much less heavily populated. In addition to the Africans captured, many thousands were killed resisting slaving raids.

THE ABOLITION OF THE SLAVE TRADE

The slave trade continued with little check for over 300 years. But by the early 19th century many Europeans had come to oppose it, and nation after nation passed laws against trading in slaves. Great Britain passed such a law in 1807; the United States in 1808; the French and Germans a few years later. It took longer for the use of people as slaves to be abolished, and this also happened at different times in different countries. In the United States it happened only after the Civil War of 1865.

Slavery was abolished in Cuba (by Spain) and Brazil (by Portugal) in the 1880s. However, in some parts of the world it never quite stopped.

Below Of the huge number (over 12 million) Africans shipped from Africa as slaves, probably as many as 20 percent died on the journey. They were packed on narrow bunk/shelves, often shackled, as here, and unable to move or turn. They were given poor food, ventilation was very bad, and there was no medical care. Even so, some tried to escape or take over the ships. If they were overpowered, they were thrown overboard alive.

The effects on Africa of the slave trade were equally prolonged – and they were certainly devastating. The trade caused African to fight African as slave dealers fought for a share of the market. It destroyed the traditional pattern of African life and ruined the economy of African states and kingdoms. Slave-labor made Europe richer and Africa poorer.

Because of the slave trade, there are now, in many parts of North and South America, the West Indies, and also in parts of Europe, millions of men and women of African descent. The slaves taken from Africa brought their musical tradition with them and their descendants adapted this legacy to produce the unique sound of jazz.

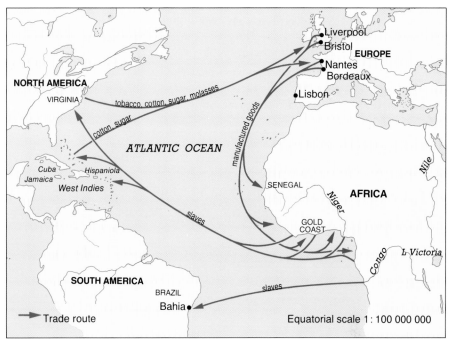

Above *At the height of the slave trade, there were three lines of trade:* Europe to Africa *Goods such as cotton cloth and firearms.* Africa to N. and S. America and the West Indies *Black slaves.* Americas to Europe *Raw goods – cotton, sugar, molasses, tobacco.*

Below *A sale of estates, pictures, and African slaves in New Orleans, North America, c. 1830.*

The African slave trade to the New World

16th century Spain and Portugal begin trade in slaves.
17th century Development of plantation slavery by Dutch, French, British. Growth of the triangular slave trade (see map).
Late 18th century Opposition to slave trade starts.
1807/1808 Slave trade made illegal in Great Britain and United States, other European countries follow.
1833 Slaves in all British possessions freed.
1830–50 Arabs start new wave of slave trade in East Africa. Continues at least until 1870s.
1861–65 American Civil War fought mainly over issue of slavery.
1880s Slavery abolished by most countries and slave trade dies out in the Americas.

THE GREAT TREK

FROM 1632 EMPLOYEES OF THE DUTCH EAST India Company, which dealt with trade between The Netherlands and its colonies in the Far East via Africa, began living at the Cape of Good Hope. Inland they knew of vast tracts of land that were sparsely populated by Africans. Some of them began to move out of the small area that the Company governed. Its administration let them take up vast areas of land for a very small fee, and soon they felt that this was their right. As numbers increased, the Company was unable to control their actions or movements. As early as 1779 there was a small "war" between farmer settlers and Africans.

DUTCH AND BRITISH IN CONFLICT

At the end of the 18th century the Napoleonic Wars set European nations quarreling. In 1806, when the Cape became a British colony, British settlers joined the Dutch and French. The original Dutch settlers resented British rule, especially stricter laws about landholding and the treatment of African workers (slavery was abolished in Britain in 1833). They wanted more land, and freedom to

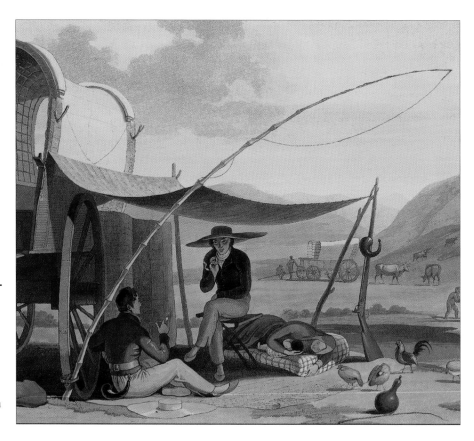

Boers in South Africa

Although opened up for white settlement by the Boer-trekkers (Voortrekkers), Natal was taken over by the British (1838), and did not become a Boer republic. All the Boer republics are now part of South Africa. Swaziland and Lesotho became independent states in the 1960s and, though economically dependent on South Africa, have remained so.

Right *After the Cape had been made a British colony in 1806, the Boers looked for new grazing lands. But the Cape's hinterland for about 625mi is too dry for good cattle and sheep pasture. The pioneer Boers, the Voortrekkers, had seen good land beyond the Orange and Vaal rivers. So it was to the high veld of the northeast that the Boers of the Great Trek of 1836 turned their oxen-teams (shown here).*

Some went east instead of crossing the Vaal, going on into Natal. There they lost more than 400 men in fighting with the Zulu chief Dingaan and his warriors. Those killed included the Trek leader, Piet Retief. Finally, in the battle of Blood River (December 1838) 3,000 Zulu died, with few Boer losses.

make their own laws. North and west of Cape Town the land was dry and barren. The best lands lay far to the northeast.

THE BOERS TREK NORTHEAST

Some pioneer Boers (Dutch for "farmer") had traveled ahead, in 1830. From 1835 Boers still in the south organized themselves into parties, and set out with their whole families and all their possessions in trek wagons drawn by teams of oxen. There were many conflicts with Africans, for much of the best land was already being used by native Xhosa, Sotho, and Zulu farmers, who also had cattle. But dangers and hardships did not stop the Boers. They crossed the Vaal and Orange rivers, and eventually formed two new Boer republics. These republics were called the Transvaal (1852) and the Orange Free State (1854).

THE ANGLO-BOER WAR

At first almost all the Boers were cattle farmers. They were hard-working people, but their lives were difficult – especially in times of drought – for men, women, and young children too. They built simple houses out of local materials, and in many ways lived much like the Africans who were their neighbors.

The Boers were determined to keep their way of life separate from the British and African peoples, and kept strictly to the teaching of the Dutch Reformed Church.

Later, gold and diamonds were found within the land that they had settled, at Kimberley and around Johannesburg. Many outsiders came to work in the mines, and the way of life began to change. This led to such difficulties that from 1899 to 1902 a war was fought between the Dutch settlers and their British rulers, which we remember as the Anglo-Boer War. It was a sad, bitter, and un-necessary war, and the memories left have caused much trouble ever since. It ended with a British victory, but in 1910 the British concluded a treaty that brought into being the Union of South Africa, uniting all the regions, including Transvaal and Orange Free State. Although they were under British rule, the Boers, known also as Afrikaners, became the dominant force in South Africa, as black people were denied voting rights.

EXPLORATION OF THE INTERIOR

THE ROUTE OF THE NILE THROUGH EGYPT had been known by Europeans for centuries. Western sailors had known the mouths of the Congo and Niger rivers for over 300 years. But in 1800 the routes of these great rivers were mostly unknown. Then, as European travelers began to move inland, the discovery of their sources became an obsession. So too did the hope of finding mineral wealth, particularly gold.

THE EUROPEAN SCRAMBLE FOR AFRICA

In the 19th century improved technology (steamships) made traveling to ports in Africa easier. New medicines reduced the risk of fever. Missionaries wanted help in ending the slave trade. Some manufacturers wanted new markets while others wanted raw materials. Some nations who had lost land in European wars wanted to gain land elsewhere. Once one nation took over a region, others wanted to do the same. National rivalry and a desire to expand trade were the main reasons for government support of exploration, although many individual explorers often had other reasons.

THE SEARCH FOR THE NILE'S SOURCE

Africans connected the Nile's source with the legendary "Mountains of the Moon." British, French, Belgian, and German explorers were all

rivals in a quest to find the sources of the Blue and White Niles. The latter held the greater mystery. The maps available were no more than guesses, and evidence for the existence of the great East African lakes was based on ancient sources and confused accounts by traders and travelers. It was finally through the journeys of a number of British explorers that the courses of both Niles were established, ending 30 years of bitter dispute and wild "scientific" claims.

Below Münster's woodcut map of Africa (1540) goes back to the map of Claudius Ptolemy (2nd century CE) and also draws on Arab and Portuguese sources. The Nile is shown rising in the far south; the upper Niger and its tributaries flow north, which is in the wrong direction.

Below Heinrich Barth (1821–65), a German, made two expeditions to Egypt in the 1840s, the first along the Nile. He led several British-sponsored expeditions into the northern regions of West Africa in the 1850s.

Left Henry Morton Stanley (1841–1904), a Welsh-born American explorer, became famous when he "found" David Livingstone, the English missionary-explorer, at Ujiji in 1871. He made several expeditions, including crossing Africa from coast-to-coast. Kasulu, his young gun-bearer, was an ex-slave whom he adopted.

Right Grant's drawing of Ripon Falls, Uganda, where the White Nile flows out of Lake Victoria. There were several expeditions (1850s–70s) to look for the source of the Nile, including those of Richard Burton and J.H. Speke. It was not until after the death of Livingstone (1873) that Stanley was able to show that the White Nile flowed from Lake Victoria to Lake Albert before continuing north into the Sudan.

Below H.M. Stanley, in 1875, approaches the dwelling of the Kabaka (king) of Buganda, a nation of the Ganda people by Lake Victoria. Stanley wrote a famous letter about the Kabaka to the Daily Telegraph. This brought British and French missionaries and later British administrators to Buganda, later a part of Uganda.

CHRISTIAN MISSIONARIES IN AFRICA

JESUS CHRIST LIVED AND DIED IN PALESTINE. In the first 500 years after the death of Jesus Christ in Palestine, Christian churches grew up in North Africa, Egypt, and Ethiopia. In the 7th century a new religion, Islam, came out of Arabia (see pages 32–33). The followers of its founder, Muhammad, destroyed the Christian churches of North Africa. Only those in Egypt and Ethiopia were left.

For nearly 1,000 years, no followers of Christ (missionaries) went to Africa. But when, from the late 15th century, Portuguese sailors and then other European travelers started to explore along the coasts of Africa and later inland, missionaries followed them.

Sometimes, missionaries themselves were the explorers. The first, Portuguese Catholic priests, worked in parts of what are now the Democratic Republic of Congo, Angola, and Mozambique. Where Dutch Protestant farmers settled at the Cape of Good Hope they taught a few Africans about Christianity.

THE MISSIONARY MOVEMENT

It was only from about the end of the 18th century that missions as we now think of them were established in Africa.

In 1799 some German missionaries went to South Africa (see page 86), and in 1804 others arrived in Sierra Leone. Roman Catholics, as well as continuing work in the old Portuguese colonies, founded new missionary orders which went to other parts of Africa. One of the most important was the Society of Missionaries of Africa (White Fathers), at first largely French, which was begun in Algeria in 1868. Italian Roman Catholics were active in the Sudan, and Belgian ones in the Democratic Republic of Congo.

Before long there were Protestant and Roman Catholic missionaries in nearly every part of Africa. As well as preaching, they began schools and hospitals and, depending on one's point of view, interfered with traditional cultural habits.

CHRISTIANITY IN AFRICA TODAY

As African churches grew, African Christians were trained as pastors and priests, and in time became the leaders of the churches. They have also started their own churches. There are now far fewer missionaries in Africa from overseas – Africans themselves are more often the missionaries.

Right A Yoruba (Nigerian) woodworker has carved the baptism of Jesus on this font. It is in the form of a traditional drum.

Below Some African Christians have begun their own churches, where they practice healing the sick by prayer. Here, a priest lays hands on a young woman to cast out the evil spirit which possesses her and causes her illness.

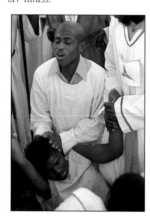

Right Christians – black and white – kneel together at Holy Communion in a church in Nairobi, Kenya.

Below A cross from the Democratic Republic of Congo, in a style that dates back to the Portuguese missionaries at the end of the 15th century.

Main European missions, 15th–19th centuries

15th–18th centuries Portuguese Catholic missionaries in Angola, Republic of Congo, Mozambique, Mombasa. **1792** Protestant Moravian Brethren to southern Africa. **1799** Protestant London Missionary Society to southern Africa. **1804** Anglican Church Missionary Society (CMS) to Sierra Leone. **1840** Catholic White Fathers in Algeria. **1845** CMS in Nigeria. **1864** Samuel Crowther, first African bishop. **1877, 1879** CMS and Catholic White Fathers in Buganda.

Mediterranean Sea

MOROCCO
1883
1859
1881
1840
1873
1840
1881
TUNISIA
1872
1884
1891
1892
1843
1879

WESTERN SAHARA (MOROCCO)

ALGERIA

LIBYA

EGYPT
1854
1882
Nile
1861

Red Sea

MAURITANIA

MALI

NIGER

CHAD
L Chad

SUDAN
1900
1899
1899
1839 ERITREA
1863 DJIBOUTI
1903
1900

1846 SENEGAL
1821
GAMBIA
GUINEA-BISSAU
GUINEA
BURKINA FASO
BENIN
Niger
NIGERIA

ETHIOPIA

SIERRA LEONE
1804
1808
1836
LIBERIA
1833
CÔTE D'IVOIRE
1913
GHANA
TOGO
1834
1842
1857
CAMEROON
1845
CENTRAL AFRICAN REPUBLIC
1913
1906

SOMALIA

EQUATORIAL GUINEA
SÃO TOMÉ & PRÍNCIPE
1848
1842
1887
1854
GABON
1874
CONGO (R.O.)
Congo
UGANDA
1879
1877
L Turkana
1910
KENYA
1900
1906

1873
1878
1866
1879
1883
1882
CONGO (D.R.O.)
RWANDA
BURUNDI
L Victoria
TANZANIA
L Tanganyika
1844

INDIAN OCEAN

1876
1869
1863

ATLANTIC OCEAN

1885
1881
ANGOLA
1888
1881
1886
ZAMBIA
MALAWI
1888
1876
L Malawi

COMOROS

1879
1886
ZIMBABWE
MOZAMBIQUE
Zambezi

1864 MADAGASCAR
1820
1867

NAMIBIA
1847
BOTSWANA
Limpopo

SWAZILAND
1816
SOUTH AFRICA
LESOTHO
1799
1823
1801
Orange
1792

--- Modern boundary

Muslim area

→ Advance of Christian missionaries

● Protestant mission with date of foundation

● Catholic mission with date of foundation

Right Reflecting the diversity of missionary teachings, the Christian churches are represented by many different denominations. The so-called independent churches are strongest in Ghana and Nigeria, Democratic Republic of Congo, Kenya, Zimbabwe, and South Africa. Since the 7th century CE Islam has dominated North Africa, Somalia, and northern Sudan. Traditional religions have little following in these areas.

Scale 1:34 000 000
0   1500 km
0   1000 miles

ISLAM IN AFRICA

THE PROPHET MUHAMMAD, FOUNDER OF Islam, was born in Arabia about 560 CE, and died in 632. Arabian Bedouin tribes had joined him in his community, and an Islamic state had been formed. After his death his disciples, with the holy book of his writings, the Koran (Qur'an) and his sayings (*Hadith*), put together the Holy Law (*Shari'a*). Assisted by Arabian armies, they extended their control over neighboring tribes and communities.

By 640 they controlled Syria and Palestine to the north, including Jerusalem. In 642 Alexandria was occupied, and in 697, Carthage. Within 100 years the peoples of the North African coast, and many of the nomadic tribes of the interior, were Muslim. The old Christian churches disappeared, although Christians and Jews, who were "people of the Book," and who, like Muslims, worshiped one god, were not forced to convert. But they had to pay a special tax, and slowly, over the years, many did in the end accept Islam. Christian churches survived only in Egypt (see pages 56–57) and Ethiopia and, for a few centuries, in Nubia (see pages 74–75).

ISLAM SOUTH OF THE SAHARA

Although the first Islamic expansion in Africa was through military conquest, since then it has usually been through trade. Muslim immigrants taught other peoples by faithfully observing their religious practices. Islam has not usually sent out special missionaries as Christianity has done: religious teachers came after a Muslim community was formed.

Islam did not cross the Sahara desert into West Africa until the 11th century. Berber tribes and traders who used caravan routes across the desert first brought it to chiefs and rulers, their subjects then copying them.

Along the coasts and islands of East Africa Islam was brought by sailors and merchants from the Middle East who settled there. The Somali tribes of the Horn of Africa and peoples of the northern Sudan and Ethiopia took up Islam through contacts with Arabia and Egypt, to their east and north.

Only in the 19th and 20th centuries did Islam expand widely in areas south of the Sahara. Even today, outside the almost totally Islamic nations (Mauritania, Mali, Niger), Islam is very much an urban religion. This is especially true in East and

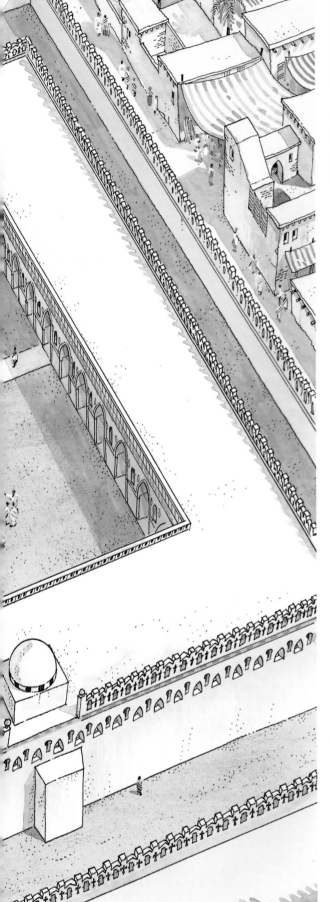

Above Mosques adapt to local building styles. This mosque, at Timbuktu, has been built from poles and mud, constructed so cleverly that the building can withstand the rare but very heavy rain. In this building, as in the most ornate or the most simple mosque, the basic rules are the same: the mihrab or niche to indicate the direction of Mecca, and the minbar for the Friday sermon.

Left The domed mosque stands in a cloistered courtyard used as a school (madrasa) where pupils are instructed in the Koran and the Shari'a. Beyond is a narrow courtyard and near the main entrance is a minaret, from which the call to prayer goes out five times each day. In a city like Cairo with several mosques this, the largest, would become the Assembly Mosque where the special Friday prayers are made. Inside there will be no pictures of people.

central Africa. Only in Tanzania are there areas where, in the late 19th and early 20th centuries, whole rural populations adopted Islam as their religion.

THE COMMAND TO PRAYER

One of the special commandments of faithful Muslims is the law to pray every day. There are two kinds of prayer. Private, personal prayer can take place anywhere at any time. But the Prophet also ordered Muslims to pray publicly, five times a day, reciting special prayers while standing or kneeling in certain ways. The believer must also have "washed" (with water or dry sand) before praying. These prayers do not need to be made at a mosque. Wherever a Muslim is, he spreads his prayer mat and turns in the direction of Mecca. (Mecca, inland from the Red Sea in Saudi Arabia, is where Muhammad was born.) But on Fridays, the special day in the Muslim week, believers go to the mosque.

A mosque is not used for ceremonies like weddings and funerals which are held in the home. In the beginning, all it needed to be was a place to meet with water for washing. But over the years some features were added. Most mosques now have a tower, a minaret, from which the mosque official calls Muslims to prayer (sunrise, noon, mid-afternoon, sunset, and two hours after sunset).

33

AFRICA'S RELIGIONS

OVER THE WHOLE OF AFRICA THERE ARE roughly the same number of Christians as Muslims, about 85 percent of Africans in total. The founders of these two religions, Jesus and Muhammad, lived in lands close to Africa. Both religions spread into North Africa and Ethiopia. In this country there has also been a community of Jews. So for many North Africans either Islam or Christianity is their traditional religion.

TRADITIONAL RELIGIONS

A "traditional religion" is usually taken to mean that followed by a particular group of people, or tribe. Before the European colonial era, traditional religions were followed by most Africans outside North Africa, Ethiopia, and a few coastal settlements. Now, about 13 percent of people follow them.

These religions have no mosques, churches, or temples. But very often there are special places, perhaps on top of a hill or under a large tree, where people gather to pray to the gods and spirits, and to make gifts to them. Usually an old man, perhaps the grandfather of the clan, acts as the priest and leads the prayers.

In some places goats, cows, or chickens are sacrificed; sometimes cooked food and beer are given as an offering. A tiny house for the spirits may be built in each family's courtyard, where food is placed (see also pages 62–63).

GODS AND SPIRITS

Old people tell the children stories about the gods and how they want people to live. Many people believe in one god, a "high god," who lives in the sky, and who was the creator of the world. Many also believe that there are spirits in trees, rivers, mountains, living creatures, and all around the village. If there is illness, or bad luck, it is often thought that it is because someone has done a wrong deed, and made one of the spirits angry. Therefore good relations between the members of a family, and between neighbors, are valued highly.

CEREMONY AND EVERYDAY RELIGION

People believe that the spirits of the dead, especially of those who have died recently, are still near them, and food and drink offerings are given to keep those spirits happy. When a new baby is born it may be given the name of someone who

Left A traditional healer has been called in to help a sick woman in northern Cameroon. Her family watch while the healer performs a ritual as she lies quietly on a mat.

Left Carving of Shango, voice and power of thunder, who was once king of Oyo. The Yoruba people revere him as a god and there are many shrines to him. Only his priests arrange burial of people struck by lightning.

Below In southern Ghana a family gathers in their courtyard to make a sacrifice of one of their animals. This is to please and show respect for their God and the spirits of the dead ancestors. The sacrifice is conducted by the clan head or, in some cults, a professional priest.

Right The Faron Mosque in Khartoum, capital of Sudan, which lies at the confluence, or meeting place, of the White and Blue Niles. This is the minaret from which the call to prayer goes out five times each day.

Khartoum was in the 1820s an Egyptian garrison town. It was here that the British soldier, General Gordon, met his death after a famous siege in 1885.

has just died. At the time of a funeral there are usually special prayers and gifts for the spirit of the dead person.

Other times when special prayers are said and offerings made to the spirits are at the birth of a child, at weddings, and at initiation rites — the times when the boys and girls come to be accepted as grown-up people in their society. In other parts of the world, too, you will notice that it is after births and deaths, and for marriages, that people most often go to a church, synagogue, chapel, or mosque.

"WITCH DOCTORS" AND HEALING

You often hear the words "witch doctor" and "medicine man" when people are talking about African religion. Some people think that they are evil people, but in fact they often are healers or fortune-tellers.

When people are puzzled about the cause of illness or bad fortune, the witch doctor tries to find the answer, so that people can get rid of the evil that caused trouble. This might be done by an offering to a spirit. People do often believe in witches, and are frightened of them, but a witch is quite different from a witch doctor, who is thought of as a healer.

Below The Friday Mosque at Mopti, southern Mali, near the Niger river. It is on an ancient caravan route. Local materials and traditional methods were used to create this truly African mosque.

Strict Muslims should pray five times every day wherever they are, but on Fridays should do so with others at a large mosque.

Women are not forbidden to attend mosque prayers, but generally they pray at home.

DISTRIBUTION OF PEOPLE IN AFRICA

THE POPULATION OF ANY PARTICULAR country or region within a country depends on such factors as physical environment, the country's history, and the economic conditions.

SPARSE AND DENSE POPULATIONS

It is not surprising that desert areas and very mountainous regions usually have low populations. The deserts of Namibia and the vast Sahara (at 3 million sq mi it is almost the size of the United States), support very few people. The same is true of high mountains, but the fertile foothills surrounding the mountains often attract dense rural populations, as in East Africa and west central Africa.

Dense populations are usually found along rivers, like the Nile, or around lakes, like Lake Victoria, which provide food as well as water. In several parts of Africa – the coasts of North Africa, along the Niger river in West Africa, in Egypt and the Sudan – large cities have existed for many thousands of years, and these cities continue to grow. But, even today, most of Africa's 500 million or more people live in the countryside, in villages, and in small towns that are market centers.

THE GROWTH OF MODERN CITIES

The existence of minerals (as in the Democratic Republic of Congo, Zambia, and South Africa) led in the 20th century to rapid growth of several large industrial cities, which attract yet more people. More than 50 million Africans now live in large cities, compared with only 7 million in the 1920s. People crowd into shantytowns where they have no proper gas, electricity, or water supplies.

Left Johannesburg (founded 1886) is the commercial and major manufacturing center of South Africa with a population of over 3 million. Far inland, the city developed around gold-mining sites. Its center looks much like that of other modern cities.

Right Xhosa men outside their huts in contemporary South Africa. The isolated village is still home to a very large number of Africans.

Early contact between white colonists and the Xhosa people led to conflict over control of Xhosa land. Nine wars were fought between 1778 and 1878.

Growth of African cities from 1300 CE

By 1300 Cairo, with 500,000 people, bigger than any metropolis in Europe or the Middle East.
By 1690 Tunis established near the ancient city of Carthage and grew rapidly under Muslim rule.
1800s In West Africa, trading towns such as Lagos, Kano, Sokoto, and Ibadan grow to population sizes of 20,000–100,000.
1880s Establishment of European colonial towns and administrative capitals – Kinshasa (1881) Brazzaville (1883), Dar es Salaam (1885), and Kampala (1890).
1910 Cape Town, the earliest European city, becomes capital of South Africa. (Population today over 1.5 million.)

Right *The largest cities in Africa today are in Nigeria, South Africa, Egypt, Morocco, and Algeria. Ethiopia has a large population but little city-development. Gabon and Namibia have small populations but great urbanization.*

- City with over 3 million people

Population per sq mi
- 260
- 130
- 26

Scale 1:62 000 000

0 — 1500 km
0 — 1000 miles

Right *The Sultan of Agades within a courtyard of his palace. The dried mud walls are built on a wooden framework and have been in constant repair since the palace was first put up in the 14th century. Agades is an oasis city in the Sahara region of northern Niger. Throughout Africa, oases – the sites of springs or wells in deserts – are the centers of dense rural populations.*

AFRICAN PEOPLES AND LANGUAGES

WHAT DO THE PEOPLE OF AFRICA LOOK like? And what languages do they speak? Each person is an individual, but there are some features that are typical of most Africans.

PEOPLES OF AFRICA

Almost everywhere in Africa, native people have dark brown or black hair, and black, brown, or yellowish-brown skins. All have brown eyes. It is the dark hair and skin color that gave us the word Negro, from Latin *niger*, which means black.

In the north, along the Mediterranean coast, most of the people are not especially different from the Greeks, Italians, and Spaniards on the north shores, with straight or wavy hair and brown skin. This shows their common ancestry. In Ethiopia and Somalia there are also people with light brown skin and wavy hair, and often sharply pointed noses.

In general, as one travels south, the people are darker, with flatter noses and with hair so strongly curled that it is called spiraled. Some are very tall, like the Dinka of Sudan, or the Tutsi of Rwanda and Burundi. Some are very short indeed, like the Mbuti pygmies of the Democratic Republic of Congo.

In southern Africa are people of different appearance. These are the Khoikhoi ("Hottentots") who were herders and hunters, and the San and other "Bushmen" peoples, who were hunter-gatherers. They have yellowish-brown skin, and softer hair. The San are much shorter than the Khoikhoi but taller than the Mbuti.

All along the East African coast there are people with lighter skin and straighter hair than the inland people. Their ancestors were both Arab and African.

LANGUAGES

There are four completely different language types in Africa:

"Afroasiatic" languages are spoken in North and northeastern Africa, and as far south as Kenya. "Niger-Kordofanian," the largest language family, includes most of the languages of West, East, central, and southern Africa. The "Nilo-Saharan" languages are spoken in the Sudan and in East Africa. The "Khoisan" languages, with their "click" sounds, are mostly spoken in southern Africa.

Within each type the separate languages (over 1,000) are related, sharing vocabulary and

Above A Kabyle man from Algeria, where Arabic is now spoken. The old Berber and Semitic languages survive only in remote rural areas.

Above A Coptic girl from Egypt, where Arabic is now the first language. Copts are descendants of ancient Egypt who took up the Christian faith.

Above In the northern Sudan Arabic is now the usual language. This woman comes from Omdurman, a city on the Nile near Khartoum.

*Below The four major language types of Africa are shown on this map. **1. Afroasiatic family** which includes Hebrew and Aramaic. It is clear that these languages, and the people who first spoke them, are linked with*

languages and peoples outside Africa. Arabic, most widely spoken, was introduced only after the Islamic invasions of the 7th century CE onward. ***2. Khoisan languages** spoken by the Khoikhoi (Hottentots) and*

the San and other "Bushmen." ***3. Nilo-Saharan** and **4. Niger-Kordofanian**. These contain the languages spoken by people who are known as typical Africans, with dark brown skin and eyes, and spiraled hair.*

Language families
- ☐ Niger-Kordofanian
- ▨ Nilo-Saharan
- ☐ Afroasiatic
- ☐ Khoisan
- ▨ Austronesian-Malagasy
- ▨ English and Afrikaans with indigenous Bantu

——— Bantu line

Igbo Separate language

Scale 1 : 62 000 000

0   1500km

0   1000miles

Above This Baulé girl, from Côte d'Ivoire, West Africa, speaks an Akan language related to Asante and Fanti (both Ghanaian languages).

Above Some sounds in the Khoisan "click" language spoken by this San girl from Botswana have been taken into the Tswana and Zulu languages.

Above This man from Mozambique speaks a Bantu language, as do most of the peoples from Kenya to South Africa and southern West Africa.

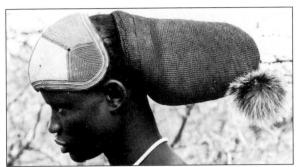

Above A young man of Karamoja, northern Uganda, who speaks the language Karamajong of the Nilo-Saharan family. It is closely related to languages spoken in the southern parts of Sudan and in Tanzania and Kenya, such as those used by Maasai and Samburu groups.

grammatical systems. The names used today for these language groups give some idea of the part of Africa where they are spoken.

On the island of Madagascar, where the population is chiefly related to Indonesia, not to the African mainland, the languages belong to a fifth type, known as Austronesian.

A WIDELY SPOKEN AFRICAN LANGUAGE

Swahili is a well-known African language. It is the "mother-tongue" of people along the coast of Kenya and Tanzania, and is also spoken by traders over most of East Africa.

Swahili (or more correctly, Kiswahili) is placed in the Niger-Kordofanian subgroup called Bantu. This name was chosen when a scholar found that in many languages (spoken from west central Africa across to East Africa and down to the Cape of Good Hope) there was a word like *bantu* meaning "people." In Kiswahili the word is *watu*. He found that Bantu languages have many shared features.

Kiswahili has a rich vocabulary containing many words derived from Arabic, as well as some from Portuguese and English. And English now borrows words from Kiswahili. *Safari* is a Swahili word meaning journey, and comes from the Arabic *safara*, travel.

Other well-known Bantu languages include Zulu, the Shona language widely spoken in Zimbabwe, and Bemba, the language of millions in Zambia.

Today, all over Africa, European languages are learned as a second language. The most common are English and French; others are Portuguese and Spanish. In South Africa the local form of Dutch is known as Afrikaans.

Above In Ganvie, southern Benin, the local people have built houses raised on stilts in the lagoon. They use dugout canoes for getting about and transporting goods. They speak Akan like the Baulé people (see above), a Niger-Kordofanian language of the coastal regions of West Africa.

EDUCATION AND LITERACY

WHEN WE THINK OF EDUCATION, WE usually think of schools. In most of Africa there have been schools, in the usual sense of permanent places of learning, only for a short time. And it is true that literacy – being able to read and write – has only recently arrived. But this does not mean that there was no education previously, nor does it mean that, because there were no books, people in Africa did not remember the stories of the past or their history.

ISLAMIC SCHOOLS

Before Western contact, the only written languages were Arabic (in North Africa and parts of East

Left A Muslim teacher instructs his class at their evening school in a street in Kano, Nigeria. The pupils use wooden writing boards. Instruction in the Koran for boys is the main object of these Muslim schools. During the daytime boys and girls receive more formal education in schools run by the government.

and West Africa) and Amharic (in Ethiopia). Kiswahili, or Swahili (see page 39), was also written down, using the Arabic alphabet. Wherever there were Muslims, there were Koranic schools where boys could learn Arabic in order to read the Koran. This is the sacred book of Islam "given" by God to the prophet Muhammad. Unlike the Bible, the Koran is supposed to be read in its original language.

Koranic schools continue, and many children (nowadays boys and girls) attend such a school in the evening after going to a regular school during the day. There were also Islamic universities, including the world's oldest university, al-Azhar, in Cairo, founded in 973.

MISSIONS AND EDUCATION

Wherever western Christian missionaries went in Africa, their first task was to write down the local language, to learn it, and to translate the Bible and other religious books. Then they could teach new Christians to read and write. In fact, baptism was often not allowed until a person was literate, and the common word for a Christian was "a reader."

The first "bush schools" were very simple, and often the church and the school were held in the same building. Because the pupils all came from wide areas, more advanced schools were usually begun as boarding schools, and up to the present many children still board, at least for their secondary education.

TRADITIONAL EDUCATION

African boys and girls used in the past to learn skills necessary for their lives and livelihoods from their parents and families. Particular skills – metalworking and pottery – could be passed on to sons and daughters.

Many African societies also had special "camps" for boys and girls, separately, which they would go to when they were ready to be accepted as adults by the rest of the community. There the male elders taught the boys, and older women taught the girls, about marriage, social customs, the society's rules, and its responsibilities and punishments. Some of the teaching was given in the form of proverbs, stories, and songs. The history of each community was also remembered through stories and songs passed down from generation to generation.

MODERN AND ADULT EDUCATION

Today, all over Africa, there are primary and secondary schools very much like those in Europe and North America. But not all children are yet able to go to school, and usually fewer girls than boys are taught. However, in many countries most children attend primary school. Fewer children are able to continue at a secondary school.

Those who are fortunate enough to attend secondary schools may go on to attend universities or colleges of technology. African students usually learn at least one European language – mainly French or English, but also others depending on their country's colonial background – as well as one

Above These Xhosa boys are taking part in a ceremony for their "initiation" as adults. The Xhosa of South Africa, like many other peoples, have camps for the youths to prepare them for joining the adult community.

This is still an important part of village life even though many adult Xhosa now work for much of the time in industrial and urban centers such as Port Elizabeth, St Croix, Durban, and East London.

or more of the local languages.

Because most adults could not attend school as children, today, in many parts of Africa, short daily classes are arranged to teach them to read and write their own languages. Special elementary literacy textbooks are prepared, and the classes are often taught by people who themselves learned as adults. If they are able to attend regularly, adults can usually learn to read well in just a few months.

Population growth works against the efforts being made to reduce illiteracy. Another problem is that adults do not always have opportunities to practice reading and writing, and so their skills do not become permanent. Rates of illiteracy among women are always higher – sometimes two to three times higher – than among men.

AFRICAN ART

AFRICANS OFTEN DECORATE THE EVERYDAY objects they use in their homes, such as plates and bowls. They also make objects used in worship, which are valued for their appearance. In some societies — mainly those that have kings or chiefs — some objects, such as heads or figures of people or animals, are made for their appearance alone.

THE EARLIEST AFRICAN ART

Although today people are most familiar with carvings and sculpture, the earliest African art known are the drawings and paintings on smooth rock, surviving in caves and rock shelters. Thousands have been found in the central Sahara; there are many in southwest Africa, South Africa, and a few other places.

Very many of these cave drawings are of hunters chasing wild animals; others are of herdsmen with their cattle. They are mainly found in the hotter, drier parts of Africa where even today hunting and herding are important. The earliest date estimated for a Saharan rock painting is 5000 BCE. These paintings and drawings show that the Sahara was once a grassy area and that the desert sands have gradually spread north and south.

AFRICAN SCULPTURE AND CARVING

The earliest sculptures (outside of Egypt) known in Africa are baked clay (terracotta) heads found around the modern village of Nok, in northern Nigeria. They show heads and figures of humans and animals, and are dated to about 2,000 years ago. The Nok tradition of sculpture in clay influences the art of the Yoruba people centuries later. Clay figures are less common than carved wood, which is found wherever there are forests to provide wood. Drums, with carved bodies made from tree trunks, are another art form.

Objects used in the homes of kings and chiefs — stools, chairs, headrests, bowls, cups, trays — are very finely carved and decorated. Ivory, from elephants' tusks, and bone were also carved and used for smaller objects — spoons, small dishes, horns, bracelets.

In some parts of Africa utensils and figures are carved from a very soft stone called soapstone. A few ancient peoples learned to use metals, such as bronze, to make objects. These were very valuable, and chiefly for rulers or for use in religious ceremonies.

Left Not a stool, but a headrest! (It is only 8in high.) The Luba women of the Democratic Republic of Congo arrange their hair elaborately (like the women in the carving) and use carved headrests at night to protect their hairstyles. Some are made of ivory; this one is carved from wood. As well as using them at night, the Luba also use these headrests in a kind of divination or fortune-telling.

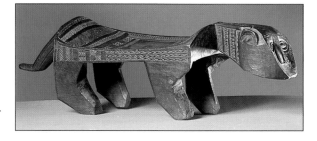

Left A headrest (6in high) in animal form from the Ngindo people, southwest Tanzania. In many societies the men wear elaborate hairstyles, fixed with mud and fibers. Often they carry the headrest on a cord around their neck.

Right The Baulé people of Côte d'Ivoire are well known for their realistic sculpture. This figure of a bearded old man is carved with great attention to detail. Note the intricate hairstyle and the gentle expression.

Below Calabashes, or gourds, which are the fruit of a vine, grow widely in Africa. When cut and dried, they are used as measures, serving dishes, food containers, and as sound boxes for musical instruments. Long thin ones are used like bottles.

These gourds, from Nigeria, have been carved with a sharp tool and dyed.

AFRICAN MASKS

In many parts of Africa members of secret societies used masks in dances at their ceremonies. These masks make up some of the most striking art in all Africa. They were sometimes carved in wood and painted, or made of skin stretched over a wooden frame. Long robes of cloth, or of grass or raffia, might hang from them and cover the whole of the wearer's body to frighten the watchers.

EVERYDAY DECORATIVE ART

Baskets are woven everywhere in Africa, and they are often beautifully decorated. Food containers and trays are carved; stools are decorated with beads and wire hammered in patterns. Earrings, necklaces, and bracelets made of metal, wood, or beads are valued for their beauty. Sometimes the walls of mud houses are used like an artist's canvas, and covered with drawings and paintings.

Where cloth is woven, it is often decorated in the process of weaving, with colored yarn used in patterns. Plain cloth is decorated by "painting on" an image or pattern in wax and then dyeing the cloth. The wax prevents the dye seeping into the cloth so that the image stays in the original cloth color while surrounding material takes up the dye.

African art is essentially a community art, hence the everyday decorative art. Only in recent years have individual artists become recognized.

Indigo dyeing

In Nigeria, Côte d'Ivoire, Senegal, and Madagascar certain plants are grown for a blue dye, indigo. Their crushed leaves are formed into balls. The blue dye is produced when the balls are soaked in an alkaline solution, made from the ash of green wood. This also "sets" the dye, to make the cloth colorfast.

Woven fabric, or skeins of cotton yarn, can now be dipped in the cold dye. The cloth or yarn is redipped several times until the right shade of blue is obtained. In Kano, northern Nigeria, the dyeing is done in vats set in the ground (left).

MUSIC AND DANCE

ALL OVER AFRICA MUSIC IS A VALUED PART of daily life. Music is made by the singing voice and by musical instruments. And with music goes dancing, because to Africans the art of music is also the art of moving to music.

WHAT ARE THE INSTRUMENTS USED?

Musical instruments vary, depending on the materials and skills available. Drums are common, but are not found everywhere, for you need large trees to make large drums – animal-skins are stretched over the hollowed trunk. Other percussion instruments are bells, xylophones, and the "thumb piano," *likembe*.

Flutes, trumpets, and other wind instruments are made from wood, reeds, or metal. Stringed instruments are often made using gourds (fruits) for the sound boxes. Even a hunting bow can become a kind of violin.

In societies where there is a king or a chief, he may have at his court an orchestra, with a singer who sings special "praise songs" in his honor. In these societies solo players of instruments may also be found, but usually in Africa everyone joins in music and dance.

Above A portable xylophone, used in Cameroon but probably coming from the Republic of Congo, to the south. A chief when traveling would take his xylophone band with him.

Right The likembe, "thumb piano," seems to come from the Democratic Republic of Congo, but has spread south to Angola, Zambia, and South Africa, and east as far as Uganda.

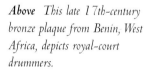

Left At the court of the emir of Zaria (northern Nigeria), an orchestra of drums, bells, and trumpets plays, while the drummer sings songs in praise of the emir.

Below In southern Angola, a hunting bow with a brace added becomes a musical instrument, played with the mouth.

Above This late 17th-century bronze plaque from Benin, West Africa, depicts royal-court drummers.

Right Dancers of the masked society, awa, among the Dogon of Mali. They appear at funerals, telling Dogon myths of life and death through dance.

Above *A masked figure from Sierra Leone, appearing in a dance of the men's society,* bondo.

Above *A masked figure appearing at the Ogun festival of the Yoruba.*

Popular African music, as played on radio throughout the continent, has traditional roots but uses modern (Western) instruments.

SINGING AT WORK AND AT PLAY

Many African songs are work songs, sung while the soil is hoed, or while grain is ground into flour, or the oars in a boat are pulled. A leader will sing a verse, and the others take up a chorus. Children have all kinds of singing games, with clapping and jumping.

American and European pop music, jazz, and rhythm and blues have all been strongly influenced by traditional African music taken by slaves to the Americas.

THE TIME OF THE FULL MOON

Moonlit nights are the time for dancing in African villages. When the drums beat people gather to dance in the open space surrounded by the houses. The dancers often wear bells and rattles at their ankles and knees. Among some peoples in West Africa and west central Africa, there are the special masked societies, whose members dance wearing masks and costumes, while others watch.

HOUSES

ALL OVER AFRICA — EXCEPT FOR THE EAST coast cities — Africans built their homes from earth, wood, and grass, and sometimes animal hides and skins. Houses built in these materials do not last long. Such houses are still being built, though stones and bricks, with cement and iron, are now used. The house may be in a village or town, or isolated in farmlands.

TRADITIONAL ROOMS AND COMPOUNDS

African houses are not usually divided into rooms, although occasionally very simple partitions are used. Each building is used for one purpose, so if another room is needed, another separate house is added. So several houses are grouped about an open space or courtyard, which becomes an open-air room where much of the daily activity goes on.

The head of the family usually has his own room. Small children mostly sleep with their mothers, and the older unmarried girls sleep in the room of their mother or grandmother. The young unmarried men generally have their own sleeping house, sometimes right away from the rest of the family. If there is a kitchen, it is used mainly as a storeroom; except during the rains cooking is done

Above The Nuba people who live in the hills of southern Kordofan (Sudan) build their thatched-houses in a ring pattern. Clay walls link the houses to form a courtyard, which has a single exit and on to which the houses open.

Right The compounds of the Nupe are built on the fertile plains near the Niger river in central Nigeria. There is a separate house for each adult member of the family; the granaries are raised on stones; there is an outer enclosing wall.

Above The Sarwa, millet farmers of Chad in west central Africa, live in villages made up of walled compounds, each of which contains one or more quite separate houses. There are narrow paths between the compound walls. The open courtyards are fenced with walls like those of the houses — either of sunbaked mud or of sorghum stalks. Here, grain and water are stored in large pots; firewood is stacked against the walls; meals are prepared out in the open.

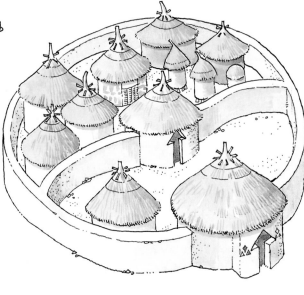

Left *A Nubian stands outside his main door. Animal and geometric patterns are drawn into the plaster, but human figures do not feature, since the Nubians are Muslims, who frown upon representations of people.*

Above *The Asante of southern Ghana build rectangular houses, joined with short walls to form a compound. Very often complicated relief patterns are drawn into the plaster. The side of the room on the courtyard is often open to the air.*

outside. In most compounds there will be separate storehouses for grains and vegetables.

BUILDING A HOUSE

Although similar materials are used all over Africa, there are many different styles and shapes – round, square, or rectangular.

The most common building method is to set straight slender tree trunks in the shape wanted, and attach a framework made of thinner more flexible poles. Then earth and water are trampled into mud in a pit, which is used to fill up the framework. This method, which is called wattle and daub, has been used by peoples all over the world.

The framework for the roof is put together on the ground before it is lifted into place, and covered with bunches of thatching grass. There are probably no windows, and just one small opening for a door. Later, the walls may be plastered with special earth, and the floor polished by applying mud mixed with cow dung, which gives a handsome finish.

Houses in shantytowns, where poor people live, are built of odd bits of timber and corrugated iron.

47

HUSUNI KUBWA

EW OLD BUILDINGS HAVE SURVIVED IN Africa because the materials (earth, wood, grass) do not last. But on the east coast, under the influence of Arab immigrants, buildings were made of more permanent materials. Some of these survived and in recent years have been excavated. They reveal much about the unique East Coast culture, which was both Islamic and African in origin.

WITH WHAT, AND HOW, DID THEY BUILD?

The Arab and African architects and builders used coral from the sea. Soft at first, this cut easily into building blocks which hardened in time. It was also ground and burned to make mortar; ground coral was used for plastering, and small pieces – coral rag – were used to fill in walls. The width of the rooms was limited by the length of the rafters; they used mangrove poles, about 8ft long. So rooms were either 8ft square, or long and narrow.

HUSUNI KUBWA

One of the most interesting group of buildings on the coast is that at Kilwa, on a headland just outside the modern town. (Kilwa is 125mi south of Dar es Salaam, in Tanzania.) The meaning of Husuni Kubwa is "large fortified house," and it must have been used as the home and "palace" of the local Muslim ruler or sultan.

Husuni Kubwa is a group of pavilions set around courtyards, on a slope. There are both public and private rooms, storerooms, an octagonal pool, and a small mosque separate from the rest but connected by a staircase. The buildings were beautifully decorated with elaborate stone carvings. There is an outer wall that seems to be part of a fortification.

Kilwa flourished in the 14th century, and one inscription found in the building names a sultan of that time. In the 15th century Kilwa declined in importance, and the ruler moved away into the town.

Right A reconstruction and ground plan of Husuni Kubwa, showing the private rooms and courtyards on the headland as well as the octagonal bathing pool, the palace courtyard, and, beyond it, the business courtyard surrounded by storerooms and with its own decorative pool. Sail-boats brought visitors and traders to the palace from ports along the East coast of Africa and Asia.

PART TWO

A REGIONAL GUIDE TO AFRICA

Above A mask of the Dan people, Liberia.

Right A camel caravan at rest, seen from a hot-air balloon, at Bilma Oasis, Niger.

Inset Key to maps in this section of the book.

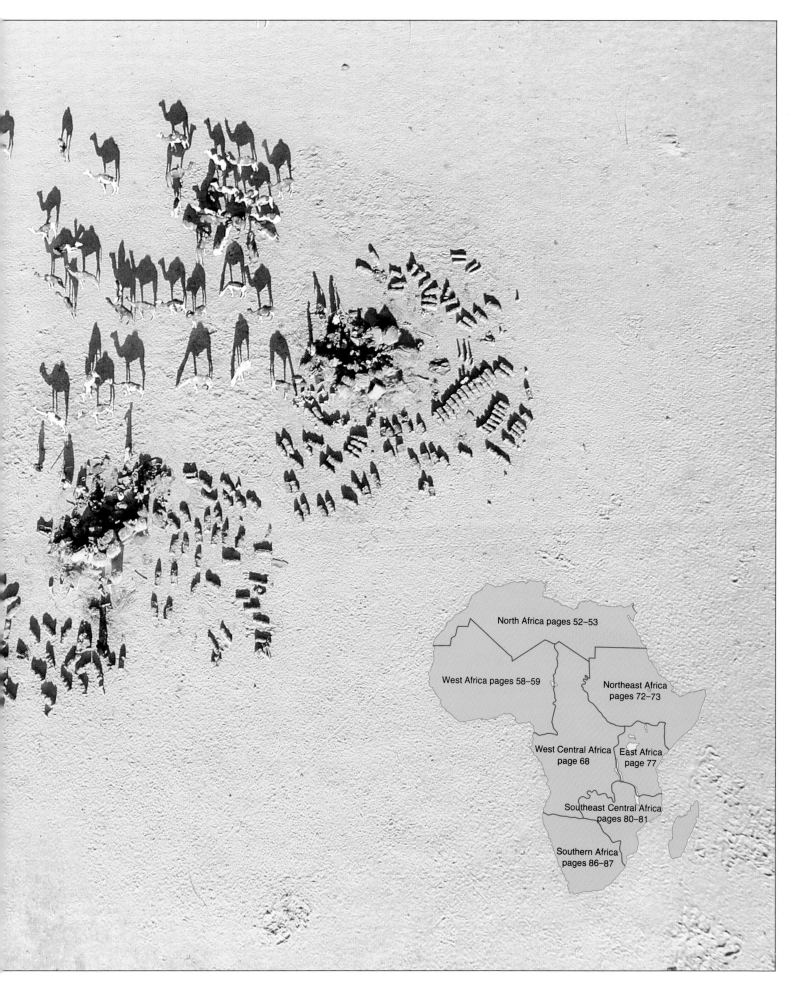

North Africa pages 52–53

West Africa pages 58–59

Northeast Africa pages 72–73

West Central Africa page 68

East Africa page 77

Southeast Central Africa pages 80–81

Southern Africa pages 86–87

NORTH AFRICA

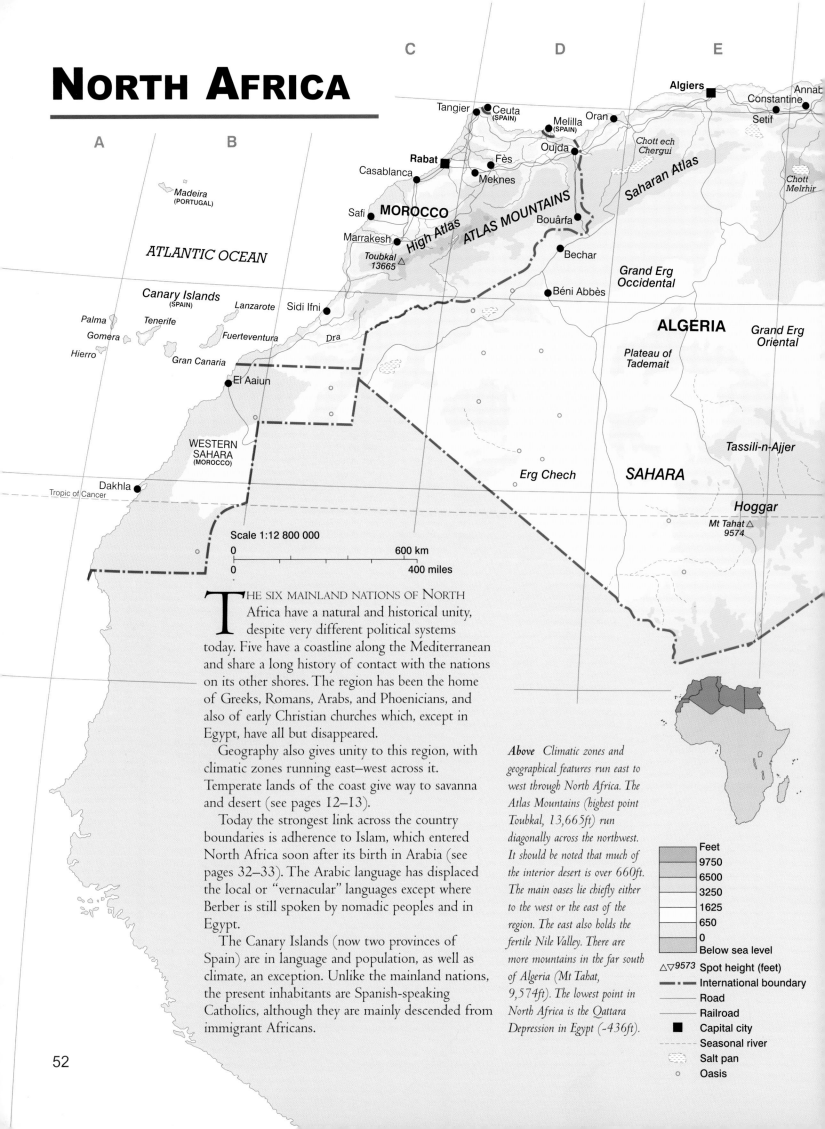

C
D
E
A
B

Algiers
Constantine
Annab
Tangier • Ceuta (SPAIN)
Oran
Setif
Melilla (SPAIN)
Rabat
Oujda
Chott ech Chergui
Casablanca
Fès
Meknes
Chott Melrhir
Safi
MOROCCO
Saharan Atlas
Marrakesh
High Atlas
ATLAS MOUNTAINS
Bouârfa
Toubkal 13665 △
Bechar
ALGERIA
Grand Erg Occidental
Grand Erg Oriental
Sidi Ifni
Canary Islands (SPAIN)
Lanzarote
Béni Abbès
Madeira (PORTUGAL)
ATLANTIC OCEAN
Palma
Tenerife
Gomera
Fuerteventura
Plateau of Tademait
Hierro
Gran Canaria
Dra
El Aaiun
Tassili-n-Ajjer
WESTERN SAHARA (MOROCCO)
Erg Chech
SAHARA
Dakhla
Tropic of Cancer
Hoggar
Mt Tahat △ *9574*

Scale 1:12 800 000
0   600 km
0   400 miles

THE SIX MAINLAND NATIONS OF NORTH
Africa have a natural and historical unity,
despite very different political systems
today. Five have a coastline along the Mediterranean
and share a long history of contact with the nations
on its other shores. The region has been the home
of Greeks, Romans, Arabs, and Phoenicians, and
also of early Christian churches which, except in
Egypt, have all but disappeared.

Geography also gives unity to this region, with
climatic zones running east–west across it.
Temperate lands of the coast give way to savanna
and desert (see pages 12–13).

Today the strongest link across the country
boundaries is adherence to Islam, which entered
North Africa soon after its birth in Arabia (see
pages 32–33). The Arabic language has displaced
the local or "vernacular" languages except where
Berber is still spoken by nomadic peoples and in
Egypt.

The Canary Islands (now two provinces of
Spain) are in language and population, as well as
climate, an exception. Unlike the mainland nations,
the present inhabitants are Spanish-speaking
Catholics, although they are mainly descended from
immigrant Africans.

*Above Climatic zones and
geographical features run east to
west through North Africa. The
Atlas Mountains (highest point
Toubkal, 13,665ft) run
diagonally across the northwest.
It should be noted that much of
the interior desert is over 660ft.
The main oases lie chiefly either
to the west or the east of the
region. The east also holds the
fertile Nile Valley. There are
more mountains in the far south
of Algeria (Mt Tahat,
9,574ft). The lowest point in
North Africa is the Qattara
Depression in Egypt (-436ft).*

	Feet
	9750
	6500
	3250
	1625
	650
	0
	Below sea level
△▽9573	Spot height (feet)
	International boundary
	Road
	Railroad
■	Capital city
	Seasonal river
	Salt pan
○	Oasis

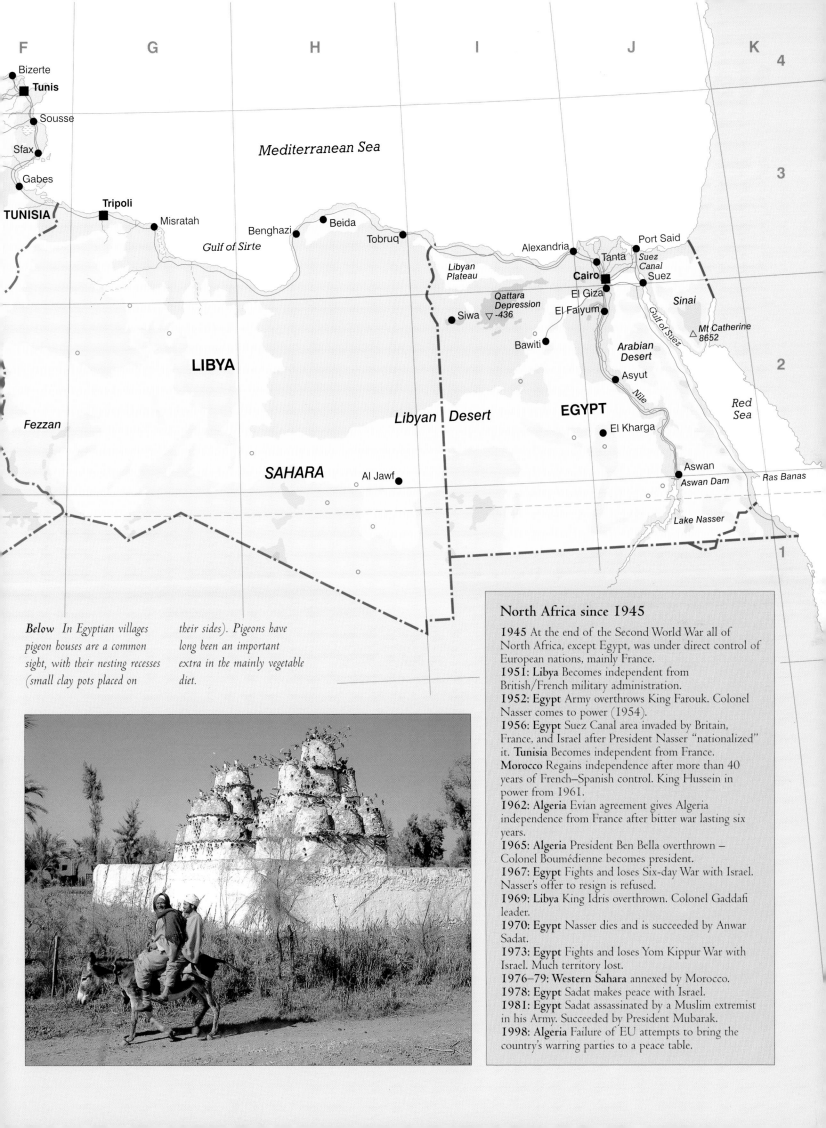

F G H I J K

4

3

2

1

Bizerte
Tunis
Sousse
Sfax
Gabes
TUNISIA

Mediterranean Sea

Tripoli
Misratah
Gulf of Sirte
Benghazi
Beida
Tobruq
Libyan Plateau
Alexandria
Port Said
Tanta
Suez Canal
Cairo
El Giza
Suez
Sinai
Qattara Depression ▽ -436
El Faiyum
Siwa
△ Mt Catherine 8652
Bawiti
Arabian Desert

LIBYA

Fezzan

Asyut
Nile

Libyan Desert
EGYPT

El Kharga
Red Sea

SAHARA
Al Jawf

Aswan
Aswan Dam
Ras Banas

Lake Nasser

Below In Egyptian villages pigeon houses are a common sight, with their nesting recesses (small clay pots placed on their sides). Pigeons have long been an important extra in the mainly vegetable diet.

North Africa since 1945

1945 At the end of the Second World War all of North Africa, except Egypt, was under direct control of European nations, mainly France.
1951: Libya Becomes independent from British/French military administration.
1952: Egypt Army overthrows King Farouk. Colonel Nasser comes to power (1954).
1956: Egypt Suez Canal area invaded by Britain, France, and Israel after President Nasser "nationalized" it. **Tunisia** Becomes independent from France.
Morocco Regains independence after more than 40 years of French–Spanish control. King Hussein in power from 1961.
1962: Algeria Evian agreement gives Algeria independence from France after bitter war lasting six years.
1965: Algeria President Ben Bella overthrown – Colonel Boumédienne becomes president.
1967: Egypt Fights and loses Six-day War with Israel. Nasser's offer to resign is refused.
1969: Libya King Idris overthrown. Colonel Gaddafi leader.
1970: Egypt Nasser dies and is succeeded by Anwar Sadat.
1973: Egypt Fights and loses Yom Kippur War with Israel. Much territory lost.
1976–79: Western Sahara annexed by Morocco.
1978: Egypt Sadat makes peace with Israel.
1981: Egypt Sadat assassinated by a Muslim extremist in his Army. Succeeded by President Mubarak.
1998: Algeria Failure of EU attempts to bring the country's warring parties to a peace table.

NOMADIC LIFE

OUTH OF THE FERTILE COASTAL STRIP WITH its good seasonal rains, a great deal of North Africa is dry and barren desert, or semidesert, with scrub and grass suitable for pasture only part of the time. This is true also of other parts of the continent – the Horn of Africa, the Kalahari Desert in southern Africa, and the Sahel which stretches across West Africa. Except at oases or along riverbanks very little can be grown in these desert areas.

THE DESERT PEOPLES

For thousands of years most of the people who have lived in the world's desert areas have been shepherds and herdsmen. Because water and grass are scarce they must move with their flocks and herds of sheep, cattle, and goats to find what they need. They are called nomads (Latin *nomas*, "wandering shepherd").

In some nations of Africa, like Somalia and Chad where drought is common, over half of the population are still pastoral nomads. As time goes on and populations grow, their number will decrease because overgrazing causes erosion leading to spread of the desert. Also, most governments prefer to govern settled populations and so encourage settlement.

THE TUAREG, NOMADS OF ALGERIA

One of the best known nomadic peoples is the Tuareg. They live in the south of Algeria and move in large clan groups across the area known as the Hoggar. No one knows very much about their origins – the leading families are brown-skinned with sharp features. Their servants are generally darker-skinned Africans.

The Tuareg are Muslims, and with them it is unusually the men, not the women, who cover their faces with a veil. They live in tents made of leather stretched across a framework of poles. Camels carry the tents and all their goods when they move.

The Tuareg stay in one place as long as there is enough water and grass. They keep goats and sheep as well as camels, but the camels are the most important because camel milk is their chief food. In some areas where settled Africans grow wheat and sorghum, the Tuareg can buy or barter their produce.

Right The Kababis of the northern Sudan are nomads who mostly use camels and, like almost all the northern nomads, are Muslim. Women weave cloth strips that are sewn together to make the tent, and make patterned carpets to sit on. The tent has an outer room for the men and their visitors, and an inner room for the women and children.

Right The Somali, another nomadic group, are found not only in Somalia, but also in the north of Kenya where they have been moving steadily for many years. Their way of life centers on waterholes.

Below A nomadic family of Bedouin, in Morocco, sit at the door of their tent as a new day dawns. They keep sheep and goats rather than camels.

CAIRO

NE OF THE GREAT CITIES OF THE MEDIEVAL and modern world, Cairo has a population in excess of 6 million. It is not as old a city as one might expect in such an ancient country.

Cairo was founded in 641 CE, when Muslim Arabs conquered Egypt. It replaced the ancient capital of Memphis, which lay 15mi to the south. Both cities are situated just above the flood level of the river Nile where it fans out into its enormous, fertile delta.

THE HISTORY OF CAIRO

As with other great capital cities that began in early medieval times, Cairo's history is firmly linked to that of the whole country. From the time the Romans were overthrown in the 7th century, Egypt was ruled by a succession of Muslim dynasties. Cairo's greatest days were perhaps under the Fatimid dynasty (970–1171) and the great Saladin of Damascus and his family and successors (1171–1516). From then until the Napoleonic invasion of 1798 its rulers were Ottoman Turks.

Modernization began in the 19th century, when first French, and then British, businessmen began involving themselves in the affairs of Egypt. Many Europeans came to live in the city, including professionals who introduced Western medicine and education. The city, which had been quite

small at the time of the French invasion, began to expand markedly from the 1830s. Today, over 15 percent of all Egyptians live there.

In 1856 the first railway (from Alexandria to Cairo) was completed, and from 1854 to 1869 the Suez Canal was built with overseas money. The ships passing through the new canal, and demand for Egyptian cotton during the American Civil War (1861–65), brought new prosperity to parts of Cairo.

Ismail, Khedive (ruler) of Egypt 1867–79, encouraged the construction of a European-style city center which still forms Cairo's hub.

CAIRO'S MONUMENTS

The enormous city, still growing, contains within itself the monuments of its long past, in its citadels, markets, tombs, and, above all, in its mosques and churches. The earliest mosque still remaining is that of Ahmed ibn Tulun, built 876–78.

Cairo, like the rest of Egypt, is mainly Muslim, but its ancient Christian church, originally a branch of the Eastern Orthodox Church, still exists. Its name, the Coptic Orthodox Church, preserves the old Roman word, Aegyptus. Its services are still held in "church Coptic." But in the rest of Africa, Egypt is known as Misri, from Misr, the original Arabic name of the settlement that became Cairo.

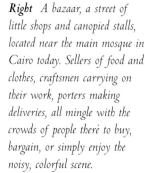

Right A bazaar, a street of little shops and canopied stalls, located near the main mosque in Cairo today. Sellers of food and clothes, craftsmen carrying on their work, porters making deliveries, all mingle with the crowds of people there to buy, bargain, or simply enjoy the noisy, colorful scene.

Left The ancient al-Azhar University was founded as a mosque that was built in 970–72 CE. Like other large mosques it became a gami'a or Assembly Mosque where theology was taught. It is now a normal university, but still trains Islamic theologians.

Right Bowls, lamps, trays, and brass or copper cooking vessels are sold in the bazaar. Traditional homes have little furniture, and large metal trays are used at mealtimes as tables placed on the floor or a low stool.

WEST AFRICA

ALL EXCEPT THREE OF THE PRESENT NATIONS of West Africa were, from the mid-19th century to mid-20th century, under French or British colonial rule. Liberia, although never a colony, has maintained close links with the United States; Guinea-Bissau and the islands that form Cape Verde were Portuguese colonies. French and English are widely spoken in West Africa.

Before the colonial period the peoples of West Africa were organized in everything from small village communities to nations and empires. Some communities follow traditional religions (see pages 34–35 and 62–63). Islam is widespread, especially in the north of the region; there are now many Christians as well. All these nations have sharp contrasts in geography and lifestyle between their fertile coastal fringe and inland semidesert.

West Africa since 1945

1945 All of West Africa, except Liberia, under European colonial rule.
1947: Nigeria Kwame Nkrumah returns to the Gold Coast. Beginning of Convention Peoples Party, first modern African political party.
1956: Nigeria Discovery of oil in eastern Nigeria. **Senegal** Granted self-government by France.
1957: Ghana First black African state given independence by Britain.
1958: Ghana All African People's Conference meets in Accra. Forerunner of Organization of African Unity (see pages 90–91). **Guinea** First French West African colony given independence.
1960: Nigeria Gains independence from Britain. **Mali-Senegal** Gains independence as short-lived Mali federation. **West Africa** All remaining French colonies gain independence.
1961: Sierra Leone Gains independence from Britain.
1966: Nigeria Parliamentary government overthrown by Army, General Gowan becomes leader in second coup. **Ghana** Nkrumah overthrown – goes into exile.
1967: Nigeria Eastern region declares itself separate country – Biafra. Civil war begins.
1970: Nigeria End of civil war – Biafra starved into submission.
1975: Nigeria Gowan overthrown. Military-dominated government keeps vast, heavily populated country together.
1982: Ghana Thousands of Ghanaian workers in Nigeria are expelled from the country. **Senegal & Gambia** The two countries join together in a federation.
1983: Upper Volta Coup brings Thomas Sanham to power. The country's name is changed to Burkina Faso.
2002: Sierra Leone General election confirms the end of the country's 11-year civil war.

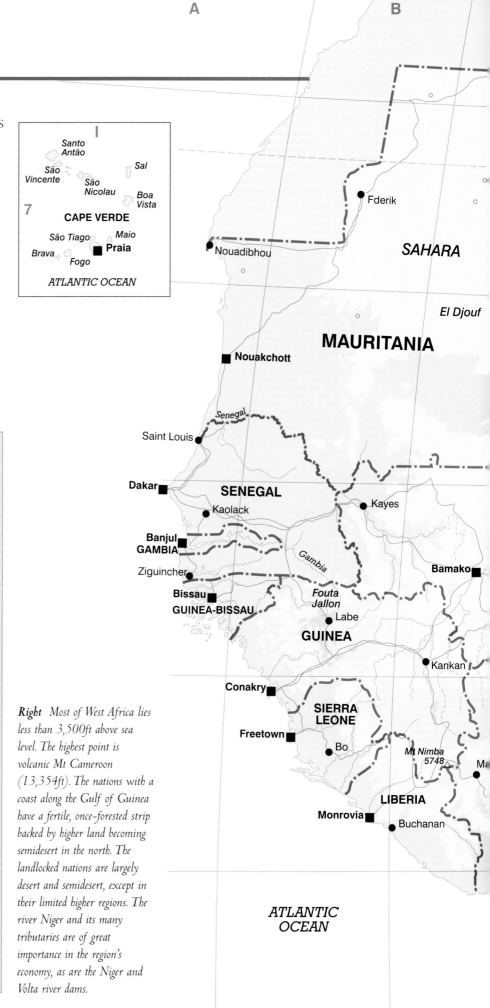

CAPE VERDE

Santo Antão
São Vincente
São Nicolau
Sal
Boa Vista
São Tiago
Maio
Brava
Fogo
Praia
ATLANTIC OCEAN

SAHARA
Fderik
Nouadibhou
El Djouf
MAURITANIA
Nouakchott
Senegal
Saint Louis
Dakar
SENEGAL
Kaolack
Kayes
Banjul GAMBIA
Ziguincher
Gambia
Bamako
Bissau
GUINEA-BISSAU
Fouta Jallon
Labe
GUINEA
Kankan
Conakry
SIERRA LEONE
Freetown
Bo
Mt Nimba 5748
LIBERIA
Monrovia
Buchanan
ATLANTIC OCEAN

Right Most of West Africa lies less than 3,500ft above sea level. The highest point is volcanic Mt Cameroon (13,354ft). The nations with a coast along the Gulf of Guinea have a fertile, once-forested strip backed by higher land becoming semidesert in the north. The landlocked nations are largely desert and semidesert, except in their limited higher regions. The river Niger and its many tributaries are of great importance in the region's economy, as are the Niger and Volta river dams.

C D E F G H

6

5

Tropic of Cancer

Feet
9750
6500
3250
1625
650
0

△13354 Mountain peak (Feet)
— ‥ — International boundary
——— Road
——— Railroad
■ Capital city
- - - Seasonal river
Marsh
○ Oasis

SAHARA

Adrar des Iforas

Djado Plateau

Air

4

MALI

NIGER

Grand Erg de Bilma

Timbuktu *Niger*

Gao

○Agades

Mopti *Bandiagara Plateau* *Sahel*

Sahel

Lake Chad

Ouahigouya

Zinder

3

Segou

BURKINA FASO

■**Niamey**

Sokoto

Katsina

Nguru

Maiduguri

■**Ouagadougou**

Kano

Sikasso

Bobo Dioulasso

Zaria

Kaduna

Maroua

BENIN

Kainji Reservoir

Jos Plateau

Garoua

Comoe

Black Volta

Tamale

Parakou

Kainji Dam

2

ÔTE D'IVOIRE

Bui Dam

Sokode

GHANA

TOGO

Ilorin

Ogbomosho

Oshogbo

■**Abuja**

NIGERIA

Ngaoundéré

Bouaké

Lake Volta

Abeokuta

Ibadan

Ife

Benue

■**Yamoussoukro**

Kumasi

Porto Novo

Lagos

Benin City

Enugu

Adamawa Highlands

oa

Akosombo Dam

Volta

Lomé

Cotonou

Niger

Onitsha

CAMEROON

Abidjan

Accra

Igbo-Ukwe

Nkongsamba

Sekondi Takoradi

Port Harcourt

Sanaga

1

Bight of Benin

Mt Cameroon △
13354

Douala

■**Yaoundé**

Gulf of Guinea

Scale 1:11 000 000

0 _____ 600 km

0 _____ 400 miles

59

A Dogon Village

THE DOGON PEOPLE ARE FARMERS WHO live in the east of southern Mali, near its border with Burkina Faso. Their home is the dry and rocky Bandiagara Plateau, within the curve of the Niger. Not far north are the deserts where nomads make a difficult living. The Dogon have apparently lived on the Bandiagara Plateau for some 500 years. They are descendants of the Tellem people, with whom they share a similar material culture.

The plateau where the Dogon live is edged with very steep cliffs, and is covered with rocky debris. Some Dogon live on the plateau, others live at the foot of the cliffs, and even on the cliffs themselves. Fertile land is precious, so every scrap is used.

CLIFF-FACE DWELLINGS

The houses, tightly grouped into family compounds, cluster together in large villages. Between the small square mud-built houses are tall tower-like granaries, or food stores, with thatched roofs. Houses and storehouses are joined with mud walls to form the compound (see also pages 46–47).

Their traditional religion is very important to the Dogon. In every village there is a *Hogon*, a priest, who leads the ceremonies and also passes on the old stories of his peoples such as how God made the world. The very way that a Dogon courtyard is arranged, its furnishings and even the position of the fireplace and entrance door and walls, serve to link the present with the past and remind the family of these stories.

CROPS AND FARMING

Despite the difficulties of their terrain, the Dogon grow enough grain for themselves and some for sale or barter. Millet is important in religious ceremonies (offerings are made at planting and harvest times). Sorghum and other kinds of grain are grown, vegetables, and where there is enough land, rice. The Dogon's plateau is not as dry as the surrounding area, and rain gets trapped in pools in the rocks. Terraces are made to grow crops, and weeds are composted to make the most of the soil.

The men like to hunt but that produces little food. Like some of their nearer neighbors, the Dogon fish or keep stock – some cattle and donkeys, but mainly sheep, goats, and hens.

Right Most daily activity in a Dogon village is in the open — houses are dark and small. Here, a man weaves cotton cloth, which is used especially for the clothes of the older men. Dyed blue with indigo, it is made into tunics and wide pantaloons. The compound elder looks on: note his cap. Dogon men almost always wear bonnets. They decorate their clothing and sandals with cowrie shells. Women wearing skirts of shop-bought cloth carry baskets of grain.

Left A Dogon village seen from a cave in the cliff-face. The flat-roofed mud houses with taller round granaries and food stores cluster together in family compounds, separated by narrow alleys. The plain beyond, once well-wooded, is now treeless.

YORUBA RELIGION

THE MAJORITY OF YORUBA PEOPLE IN Nigeria, Benin, and Togo are now Christians or Muslims, but their traditional religion has not completely disappeared. Also, because many of the slaves who were taken to the West Indies and Brazil were Yoruba, some of their old religious practices continue on the other side of the Atlantic.

THE YORUBA HIERARCHY OF GODS

The Yoruba's political system was based on a kingdom, with chiefs and a nobility, but was not very unified. Their religion though sharing features of other African religions (see pages 34–35), was diverse with four ranks of gods or spiritual beings. They numbered about 400 in all, with different places having favorite gods.

The Supreme Being is called Olorun (also Olodumare, "owner of heaven"), who holds the ultimate unity at the top. Ranked under him are subordinate gods and goddesses, *orisha*. Obatala, the god of creation, is the most important of these gods.

In the third rank are the spirits of great ancestors, humans who have become gods. There is Shango, god of thunder, and — most effective and widely found — Ogun, god of iron and war. Then there are the spirits connected with the earth (Ile), and also rivers, mountains, and trees.

Olorun, the Supreme Being, is seen as immortal, all-knowing, all-powerful, and totally just. Prayers are made to him, but there are no shrines in his honor. It is thought that the subordinate gods and the other spiritual beings who have shrines dedicated to them will pass on any offerings. Many rituals end with the words: "May Olorun accept it."

A shrine may from the outside look like an ordinary Yoruba house, but contains carvings representing the gods to which it is dedicated. Inside, priests wait for those who bring offerings to the gods or come to consult.

PRAYER, WORSHIP, AND MASQUERADES

Men and women pray to the gods in private, and join with others to worship them. The Yoruba, like most African peoples, respect ancestors and make sacrifices to them. Dogs, for example, are sacrificed to Ogun.

The Yoruba have highly developed forms of "divination" (finding out about future events).

Above Masked dancers at Egungun perform when the spirit of a dead person "visits." Every part of the dancer's body must be hidden or the spell will be broken. Masks are often of animal heads and clothes are richly decorated.

Above Some nature spirits are male, some female. Not all are good: Oya, goddess of the river Niger, brings strong gales. This goddess, Yemoja, is good: she is the goddess of water, rivers, and streams and is seen as the source of all life-giving water.

Above Shango, the powerful god of thunder, was once a fierce Oyo king. Gifts are made to him so that he will not destroy houses and men. Shrines to Shango are also found in North and South America and the West Indies.

When they are puzzled about which course of action to follow they will ask a priest. He may, for example, consult the way palm nuts lie on a special tray. The Yoruba may also consult an "oracle," by questioning a god or spirit at a shrine, again through a priest or diviner. There was an especially famous one at Ife, the religious heart of Yorubaland. Special objects in the Yoruba system of divination include a bell, made of wood or ivory, used to summon the oracular spirit, and lots, which may be core shells or animal teeth.

Part of Yoruba worship is special dances, some of them masquerades, or masked dances, that bring the people together to honor the gods and spirits. Most of the dances are important in showing respect to the dead and keeping health and harmony among the living.

One famous masquerade is Egungun, where the ancestor's spirit returns to the community to visit his "children." Dancers are clothed in materials that are whirled about in changing forms, making the ancestors "manifest," or appear.

Another dance, *gelede*, danced in western Yorubaland, is performed to entertain and please the malign (bad) spirits or witches so that they will not harm the community.

Above Carved figures of Eshu the trickster god, the messenger between gods and men who can do both good and evil. No traditional believer fails to make gifts to him. One of this pair of figures is male, the other female, underlining the different forms in which Eshu appears.

Right Some gods are local; others, like Ogun, are known throughout Yorubaland. Sacrifices to Ogun are made everywhere. He helps hunters, blacksmiths, butchers, and barbers and, nowadays, truck and taxi drivers. It is by Ogun that traditional believers take an oath in court.

Left In Yorubaland priests are attached to temples and shrines erected in honor of the subordinate gods, ancestor gods, and the nature spirits, whose images are kept in the shrines. After training, the priests are recognized as competent to offer the sacrifices, usually goats or chickens. Some priests also act as diviners.

ASANTE CEREMONIAL REGALIA

THE KINGDOM OF ASANTE, IN THE MODERN state of Ghana, became powerful in the early 18th century. At that time, its Asantehene (king), Osei Tutu, decided to strengthen the power of the kingdom. Together with his chief priest, Osei Tutu made changes to the constitution (the laws by which a country is governed), and made changes to the ceremonial regalia, particularly the royal stool.

In Asante, as elsewhere in West Africa, the king was generally regarded as the link or intermediary between heaven and earth. Up until Osei Tutu's time, the royal throne (a stool) had symbolized the

Right *Chiefs with their wives and attendants await the Asantehene. A musician plays a side-blown horn.*

Below *Chiefs holding gold-plated state swords and protected by umbrellas attend the funeral of Asantehene Sir Agyeman Prempeh II (1970). In the late 1930s he did much to restore the glories of the old ceremonies.*

Above *Chiefs wearing their ceremonial gold-plated headdresses. Their robes, sewn from narrow woven strips, are worn thrown over one shoulder.*

Below *Musicians playing side-blown ivory horns at an Asante state ceremony. Each chief has his own horn-blower who sounds an individual note. This* note identifies the chief and tells his people of his arrival. Each horn has its own name. Drums and gongs are also used in the ceremonies.

individual ruler. Osei Tutu substituted for it a special Golden Stool, which he said had descended from heaven into his lap, symbolizing the Asante nation. Thus, even when the ruler died the nation would live on in the stool.

THE ODWIRA FESTIVAL

Every year the people of Asante assembled after the yam harvest for a national festival, the Odwira. This festival was to honor the nation, and so remind the people of their unity with their kingdom, and also their unity with their spirit ancestors. Cleansing rituals, called "purificatory ceremonies," linked the living and the dead.

The Golden Stool was hung with the golden death masks of enemy generals who had been defeated by Asante armies. During the festival it was carried in procession and placed on a throne, without ever touching the ground.

The royal power was also shown in the regalia – cloths, ornaments, and decorations – worn or carried by the Asantehene and his chiefs. Vast umbrellas topped by golden ornaments shielded them from the sun, and they wore gold rings and headdresses, and carried gold-plated swords.

Since Asante lies in a gold-bearing region and gold has been important for her trade, the Odwira Festival with its very visible use of gold gave a sense of wealth, dignity, pride, and above all unity throughout the various Asante groups that made up the kingdom.

THE BRITISH ASSUME CONTROL

As Britain extended its power in West Africa, there were clashes with the Asante and the area became a British protectorate in 1896. Britain wanted more control over the West African coast in order to protect its valuable trade. As early as 1874 the capital of the Asante kingdom, Kumai, had been sacked. Later, the king, Prempeh, was removed, and by 1901 the area was annexed with the southern area of what is now Ghana as the colony of the Gold Coast.

The British administrators, knowing but not understanding the power of the Golden Stool, continued to use it, often in ways that distressed the people of Asante.

In 1935 the Golden Stool was given back to the Asante people and a new Asantehene, Prempeh II, revived the ceremonies. Thus the Asante were once more united, at least in a symbolic way.

NIGERIAN ART: BRONZE-CASTING

Throughout Nigeria there has been a long tradition of producing bronze statues, masks, and ornaments. There seem to have been many centers of production.

At Benin, a highly developed culture flourished in the 16th and 17th centuries before the slave trade caused a long decline. As well as bronze- and brass-casting, the Benin arts of fine ivorycarving and woodcarving are also renowned. When the palace of Benin was looted by the British in 1897, great numbers of very high quality bronze sculptures were taken (most are now in British and German museums). A British official described what was stolen as "a regular harvest of loot!"

AN INCOMPLETE HISTORY

From the 1920s quantities of metal objects were found in southeastern Nigeria, often at places where there was no tradition of metalwork. The history of Nigerian bronze-casting is far from complete. A new discovery could easily change the picture.

Most of the huge number of metal objects known have been found accidentally – like the hoard excavated by Thurston Shaw at Igbo Ukwe (near Onitsha) in 1937 or, in the same year, the Ife bronzes, found near the palace of Ife. They are surely only a small part of what must have existed.

Above This fine figure of a dwarf is one of the most lifelike found at Benin. It belongs to the earliest period (16th century) and is close in style to the Ife tradition. Ife is thought to have been the original home of the technique of bronze-casting.

Left A plaque from the palace at Benin City. A 17th-century Dutch traveler described the palace as having "wooden pillars encased in copper, where their victories are depicted." This plaque from such a pillar shows hunters and leopards against a background of leaves.

Right Also from Benin is this superb bronze ram's head. It probably dates from the 17th century and was an ornament on a belt worn by a chief. Most bronzes from Benin seem to have been for ceremonial use or for the ornamentation of the leading people.

METHODS OF BRONZE-CASTING

Bronze is an alloy of copper and tin – if zinc is used with the copper, brass is the result. If lead is added, the alloy is more easily worked. Lead, tin, and zinc are all found in Nigeria; copper was imported, perhaps from Niger.

Most Nigerian bronzes were produced by a process known as the lost wax method. A clay core (an exact model of the final object) was covered with a layer of wax, and then with a layer of clay, making a kind of sandwich. The result, the cast, was held in place with iron pins and sun-dried. The wax or latex was then melted out through holes left in the outer clay covering and replaced by molten bronze. When the metal had hardened, the outer clay was removed to reveal the bronze sculpture.

BRONZE-CASTING AT BENIN AND IFE

Benin City was by the 15th century the center of a powerful state in the forest area west of the Niger

delta. Up to the present there has been a continuous history of brass-casting. At Benin the industry seems to have been at its height from the 16th to the 19th centuries.

Northwest of Benin, at Ife, the exquisitely fine, naturalistic bronze heads date back as far as the 12th century. These probably also relate to Nok terracotta (earthenware) sculptures which go back for another 1,000 years.

An amazing number of skills must have existed among local peoples for such bronzes to be produced. First the modeler or sculptor has to produce the clay and wax core, then the metal-casters set to work. When the metal object is broken out of its clay case, it has to be filed down, smoothed, and finished.

When we add to this the transport and production of the ores, it is clear that such work would only be produced in a prosperous and stable society, usually with a king or chief who was the sponsor, or patron, of the industry.

Left One of a group of bronzes from the lower Niger. Full of lifelike detail, it shows a hunter returning home with an antelope slung over his shoulders, its legs tied.

Below A horse and rider with elaborate headdress, in the rather stiff, court style of the mid-17th century. Bronze-casting in Benin was under the direction of its Oba (ruler).

W. Central Africa

ALL THE NATIONS OF WEST CENTRAL AFRICA were at some time colonies of France, Spain, Belgium, or Portugal. There is an immense geographical range, from the tropical rainforests of the Democratic Republic of Congo and Gabon through grasslands to the desert of northern Chad. Ways of life are as varied as the landscapes.

DIFFERENT PEOPLES AND CULTURES

In the northern deserts of landlocked Chad are nomadic pastoral peoples who are Arabic-speaking Muslims. Most people, however, follow traditional religions and a number are now Christians. The people of this region outside the desert areas mainly combine agriculture with keeping stock or, especially in the Democratic Republic of Congo, with fishing.

In the forests are small people, pygmies, who are hunter-gatherers (see pages 70–71). They were living in the region long before the majority population of Negroid agriculturalists, Bantu-speaking peoples, who are thought to have arrived from the 10th to the 14th centuries. The pygmies' own language has long since disappeared and they share local languages and exchange goods with these farming peoples.

It is believed that the Bantu-speaking peoples spread out from these forests, eventually migrating

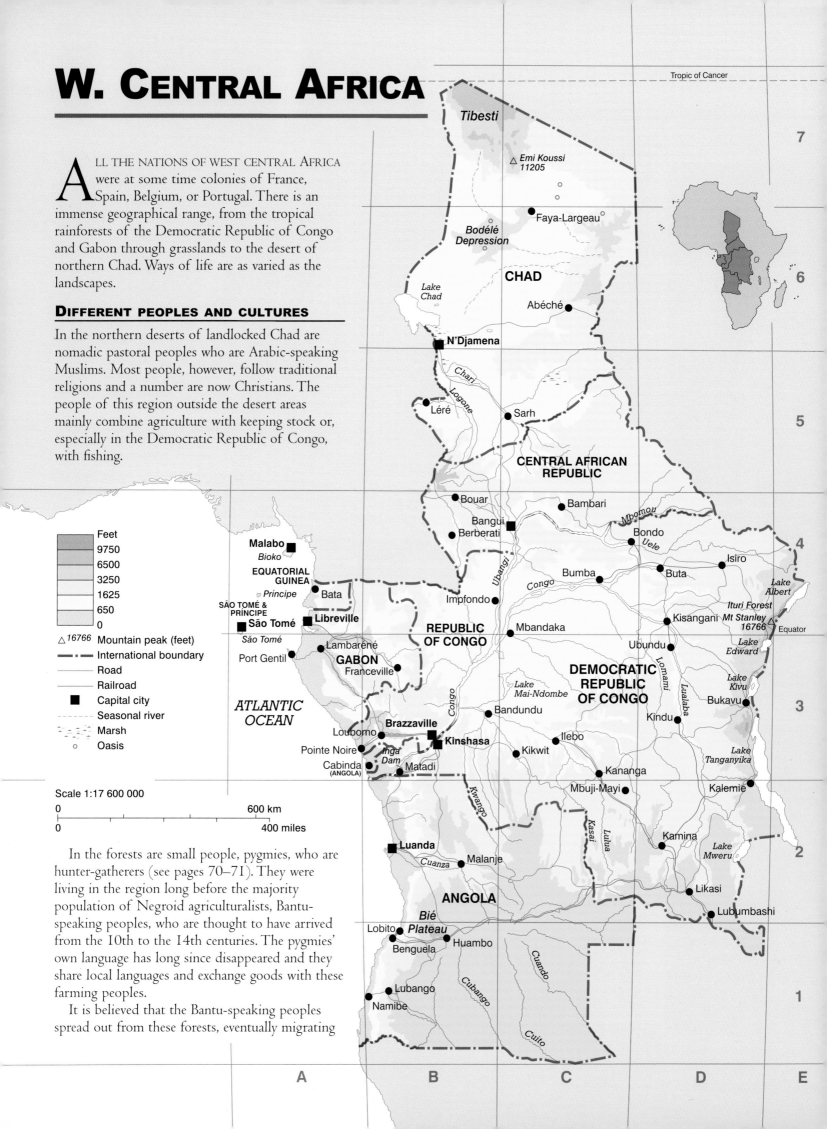

Tropic of Cancer

Feet
9750
6500
3250
1625
650
0

△ 16766 Mountain peak (feet)
—·—·— International boundary
———— Road
———— Railroad
■ Capital city
- - - - - Seasonal river
  Marsh
○ Oasis

Scale 1:17 600 000

0 — 600 km
0 — 400 miles

Right A manganese mine at Moanda, near Franceville, in southeastern Gabon. Minerals such as manganese and uranium are bringing prosperity and change to Gabon, the Republic of Congo, and other countries of west central Africa. Gold, diamonds, and iron ore are exported from nations in this region. The south of the Democratic Republic of Congo has great mineral resources.

Right Fulani (Fulbe) people are found across West Africa from the Atlantic to southwest Chad. They do not speak Bantu but Nigritic. Many are Muslim. They vary greatly in appearance and in their way of life; a large number are nomadic.

Left There is great geographic diversity in this region, which stretches from the Tropic of Cancer across the equator to 18°S. The area covers the desert of inland Chad, the plains and high plateau of Angola (where cattle can be raised), and the vast plateau of wooded savanna and the forested river valleys of the Democratic Republic of Congo. The rivers provide a means of communication and an important food source.

Left In southern Chad, near Léré, the main agricultural region of the country, villagers store their grain (mainly millet) in tall granaries made of clay and designed to keep out pests such as rats.

into East and southern Africa. South of the Central African Republic most people speak Bantu languages. (French and Portuguese are the most widely-spoken second languages.)

Political organization in this region before modern times varied from the tiny bands of the pygmies to chiefdoms or kingdoms such as Kongo, Loango, and Ndongo. Large village settlements, or small towns, with the houses laid out in regular rows, are common, in contrast to the rather less regular groupings found in North or East African villages.

Cotton, coffee, rice, rubber, and oil palms are all grown. Several of the nations have oil reserves, and the Democratic Republic of Congo is especially rich in minerals. In the extreme southeast, on its border with Zambia, it forms a part of the Copper Belt (see pages 84–85), and it exports other minerals (tin, gold, manganese) and also diamonds.

Since independence there has been a good deal of political instability in all these nations except the three smallest states – Gabon and Republic of Congo (both formerly part of French Equatorial Africa), and Equatorial Guinea (formerly Spanish Guinea). Angola, which was poorly developed by Portugal, only achieved a shaky independence in 1975.

West central Africa since 1945

1944–45: Brazzaville (**French Congo**) Conference maps out future for French colonies in area.
1960: **Chad, Central African Republic, Gabon, Republic of the Congo** (formerly French Congo), **Belgian Congo** Become independent. **Belgian Congo** Quickly descends into civil war as Katanga, its richest region, secedes (withdraws).
1965: Belgian Congo General Mobutu overthrows civilian government. Rules in personal style but brings stability. **Central African Republic** Colonel Bokassa comes to power. Later declares himself emperor and begins reign of terror.
1968: Equatorial Guinea Gains independence from Spain.
1971: Belgian Congo Changes name to Zaïre.
1975: Angola Becomes independent from Portugal but civil war breaks out.
1983: Chad French soldiers sent to Chad to fight against Libyan-backed rebels.
1996: Chad Peace terms agreed and new multiparty constitution created.
1997: Zaïre Mobuto flees after rebellion. Country is renamed Democratic Republic of Congo.
2002: Angola Africa's longest-running civil war ends.

A PYGMY ENCAMPMENT

LEGENDS OF PEOPLE ALL OVER THE WORLD mention "little people" – dwarfs, pixies, or fairies. In some parts of Africa there are people who are smaller in height than their neighbors, and who follow a different way of life.

In Kenya and in Tanzania the Dorobo and Kindiga peoples who live among the Maasai are hunters and not cattle keepers, and are generally smaller and quite different in appearance from all their neighbors. The Kindiga speak a different language. In the tropical rainforests of the Democratic Republic of Congo are people of short stature. Europeans called them pygmies from the Greek word meaning "undersized."

PYGMIES OF THE ITURI FOREST

There are a number of groups of such people in the rainforests, and they live by hunting and by gathering forest plants and fruit. Their origins are unknown. We know most about the Mbuti of the Ituri Forest, in the Democratic Republic of Congo. Adult men average less than 5ft in height, and they are slightly built, light brown in skin color, but otherwise not very different from their taller neighbors. They have no chiefs, but live in family groups joined in small bands, and move often to hunt and gather food. For huts or shelters they build dome-shaped frameworks of saplings covered with leaves. Their clothing was traditionally made

Below A clearing in the rainforest where a band of pygmies have set up their encampment. A man prepares for a hunt armed with bow, arrows and net, while a woman returns with fruit. Traditional bark cloth is being prepared by beating bark with a stone mallet, and a mother adorns her child with dye.

Above In the clearing around their shelters, a band of pygmies perform a ceremonial dance. Here, their clothing is made from bunches of leaves. These pygmies live in the far north of the Democratic Republic of Congo.

from skins or from bark cloth. The men hunt with spears, and bows and arrows, and also trap small game in nets made of twine.

All the Ituri Forest pygmies have a strong belief in a "high god," a good and kind god of the forest, to whom they pray and make sacrifices. They believe that they please their god by living in harmony with the forest. If they once had their own language, it is now lost. All the pygmy groups now speak the Bantu language of their farming neighbors. They also obtain goods that they need from these people. Grain and vegetables are not readily available to the pygmies, so they obtain these in exchange for meat, bone, and ivory.

NORTHEAST AFRICA

THIS REGION IS SOMETIMES KNOWN AS THE "Horn of Africa." Its people in Djibouti, Somalia, and eastern Ethiopia are Muslims, and mostly live as nomadic herders struggling against a harsh climate. Although the nomadic tribes are often at war, they have much in common in their culture and way of life. Sudan and the rest of Ethiopia present great contrasts within themselves and with the eastern region.

Sudan is very much a bridge between the lighter-skinned peoples of Islamic Africa to the north and darker-skinned non-Muslim people in its own southernpart (although here many of those who followed traditional religions are now Christian or Muslim).

Ethiopia is an exception to almost all general statements about Africa. Within its mountainous highlands live peoples who have for centuries been either Christians, Jews, or Muslims. Here too are found followers of traditional religions and others who only recently converted to Christianity.

Britain and France were the main colonial powers in the Sudan, Somalia, and Djibouti. Italy ruled a part of Somalia and for a few years (1936–41) Ethiopia, which had kept its independence for centuries. In some form Ethiopia has had a continuous existence for 2,000 years.

Northeast Africa since 1945

1945: Somalia South Somaliland returned to Italy by Britain.

1952: Ethiopia Eritrea (former Italian colony) joined to Ethiopia by United Nations.

1956: Sudan Gains independence from Britain. Civil war between Christian South and Muslim North until 1972.

1960: Somalia Italian and British Somalilands join together as one independent country.

1963: Ethiopia In Addis Ababa the Organization of African Unity (OAU) is formed at a meeting of all independent African states.

1969: Somalia General Siad Barre becomes head of state.

1974: Ethiopia Emperor Haile Selassie overthrown. Empire abolished.

1975: Ethiopia Colonel Mengistu comes to power. Allies Ethiopia to USSR. Rebellion in Eritrea gathers force.

1977: Djibouti Gains independence from France.

1983: Ethiopia Drought and war with Eritrea causes one of worst famines ever known. Millions die in spite of massive food and medical aid from Europe and America.

1993: Eritrea Independence of Eritrea recognized.

2002: Sudan Southern rebels continue to press for independence from the North.

Right Stretching inland from the Horn of Africa and the Red Sea, this is a region of contrasts. Most of the Sudan, and almost the whole of Somalia, is low, hot and dry, while Ethiopia is largely high plateau with highlands over 6,600ft and many peaks over 13,000ft. In the south of Sudan along the White Nile are the huge Sudd swamps, where masses of vegetation restrict river transport. The White Nile originating in Uganda and the Blue Nile from Ethiopia meet at the capital city of Sudan, Khartoum.

Left The Shilluk people of the southern Sudan choose a reth (king), who represents their divine hero-god Nyikang. Here, at the coronation of a new reth, an effigy of Nyikang, made of ostrich feathers, is carried on a 10-day procession to the town of Fashoda.

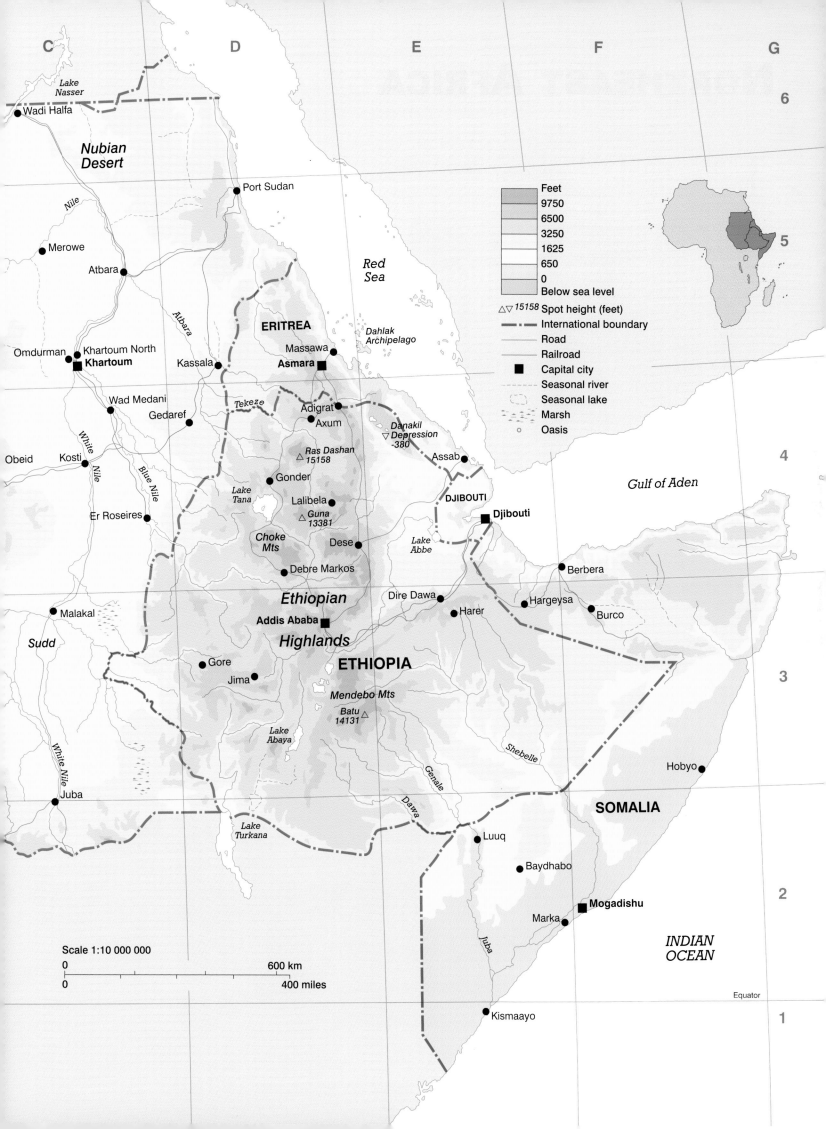

C   D   E   F   G

6

*Lake
Nasser*

● Wadi Halfa

*Nubian
Desert*

● Port Sudan

*Red
Sea*

Nile

5

● Merowe

● Atbara

ERITREA

Massawa ●

*Dahlak
Archipelago*

	Feet
	9750
	6500
	3250
	1625
	650
	0
	Below sea level

△▽ 15158 Spot height (feet)
— · — International boundary
——— Road
——— Railroad
■ Capital city
- - - - Seasonal river
Seasonal lake
Marsh
○ Oasis

Omdurman ● ● Khartoum North
■ **Khartoum**

Kassala ●

Asmara ■

Adigrat ●

4

Obeid ● Kosti ●

*White
Nile*

● Wad Medani

Gedaref ●

Tekeze

Axum ●

▽ *Danakil
Depression
-380*

Assab ●

Gulf of Aden

● Er Roseires

*Blue
Nile*

*Ras Dashan
△ 15158*

Gonder ●

*Lake
Tana*

Lalibela ●

△ *Guna
13381*

DJIBOUTI

■ **Djibouti**

● Berbera

*Choke
Mts*

Dese ●

*Lake
Abbe*

● Debre Markos

Ethiopian

● Malakal

Sudd

Dire Dawa ●

● Hargeysa

● Burco

Addis Ababa ■

Highlands

Harer ●

3

● Gore

ETHIOPIA

Jima ●

Mendebo Mts

*Batu
14131* △

*Lake
Abaya*

Shebelle

● Hobyo

White Nile

● Juba

Genale

Dawa

SOMALIA

2

*Lake
Turkana*

● Luuq

● Baydhabo

Marka ● ■ **Mogadishu**

Juba

*INDIAN
OCEAN*

Scale 1:10 000 000

0

0

600 km

400 miles

Equator

● Kismaayo

1

CHRISTIANS IN ETHIOPIA

THERE HAVE BEEN CHRISTIANS IN PARTS OF what is now Ethiopia (the old kingdom of Axum) since the 4th century CE, and at that time Christianity became the state religion, although it was probably a minority religion until the 12th century. It was the most southern of a series of Christian countries that stretched south along the Nile.

From the 9th century, as with nearly all the other Christian kingdoms of North Africa and the Nile, the Ethiopian Church came under threat from Islam. However, the mountainous terrain which has always kept much of Ethiopia isolated allowed it to survive although in a weakened form.

Relations were kept up with the Ethiopian Church's nearest Christian neighbor, the Coptic Church of Egypt, although the two differed in teaching. In fact until 1950 the Archbishop of the Ethiopian Orthodox Church was an Egyptian, appointed by the Orthodox patriarch of Alexandria.

THE ADMINISTRATION OF THE CHURCH

The Ethiopian Church retains many features of other eastern churches, such as a dual clergy of priests and monks. The Ethiopian Church is led by an archbishop (the Abuna) and bishops (churches

of this kind are called "episcopal"). Under them are priests and deacons (*dabtara*). Some priests marry; others remain unmarried and are monks. Before a man becomes a priest, he must be a *dabtara* for a while; some *dabtara* never become priests, but work for the church as musicians, teachers, and clerks.

It is the priests who lead the worship and who take services for baptism, holy communion, marriages, and funerals. Only the unmarried priests can become bishops. In their services the priests use the old Semitic language, Ge'ez, from which the Amharic language, now used every day, descended.

Left Education for the service of the church, including the reading of Ge'ez, usually takes place in monastery schools. Here a young deacon learns from older clergy in a monastery in Axum, Tigre. In the Ethiopian Church it is common for the deacons to be better educated than the more senior clergy.

Below An Ethiopian priest, in his ceremonial robes, holds two of the hand crosses that are carried in procession. Crosses of every kind are a special feature of the Ethiopian Church; they are worn around the neck, carried, painted, and embroidered. Some Christians even have a cross tattooed on their wrists or forehead, a sign that cannot be removed.

Left The cross-shape of St George's Church and the three crosses carved on its roof show clearly. These rock churches are built by digging a deep trench, and then excavating within the block. The trench round this 13th-century church is 62ft by 76ft, and it is about 40ft deep.

Left Another view of St George (Beta Giyorgis) at Lalibela. The church rises 36ft from the rock base out of which it is hewn.

Right In many Ethiopian churches there are murals telling stories from the Bible or from the lives of saints. Here St George, killing the dragon, is shown with a group of Ethiopian cherubs (at Lake Tana, to the west of Lalibela).

TEACHINGS AND FESTIVALS

In most respects the teachings of the Ethiopian Church are very close to those of the other eastern (Orthodox) churches, and especially to the Coptic Orthodox Church of Egypt. But it has kept some customs similar to Judaism, and some which probably continue parts of the old pre-Christian traditional religions. These include the keeping of the Sabbath as well as Sunday, circumcision for all males, laws about purification and cleanliness, and animal sacrifices. The Ark of the Covenant is given an important place in every church. Apart from services held on the Sabbath (Saturday) and Sundays, special festivals like Christmas and Easter are kept. One great festival is that of the Baptism, when the people go in procession to a lake or river. The priest blesses the water and the people bathe in the water, so recalling their own baptism.

At the festivals the *dabtara* play musical instruments (harps, rattles, and drums), and each priest beats the rhythm with a special baton called a prayer stick.

THE GREAT STONE CHURCHES

In the 12th century, King Gadla Lalibela began to build wonderful churches at a place which is now called Lalibela, after him. Lalibela is a remote mountain village in Welo Province, north of Addis Ababa, but it was once the capital of Ethiopia. King Gadla Lalibela may have begun his church-building to make his rule acceptable and certainly to enhance his city.

The churches were cut out of a soft volcanic rock called tufa, which hardens after cutting. Full of paintings and carvings, they are a wonderful exhibition of a church that has continued for 16 centuries despite every possible kind of difficulty.

Above A rock-cut path to one of the churches at Lalibela, itself carved out of the rockface. The pinkish color of the soft tufa rock may be clearly seen. The largest of these rock churches is Beta Madhane 'Alam, "House of the Redeemer of the World," which is 110ft long and 38ft high.

EAST AFRICA

BEFORE THE FIRST WORLD WAR EAST AFRICA was under either British or German colonial rule. After the war the area known as German East Africa became Tanganyika, a British colony. The two small kingdoms of Rwanda and Burundi became Belgian colonies. Uganda, Kenya, and Zanzibar continued under British rule. Since the Second World War all these countries have become independent.

In the north and northeast of Uganda and Kenya, along the coasts and in some parts of Tanzania, Islam is strong. Inland, most regions have large Christian communities, with others following their traditional beliefs.

Languages of several families (such as Luo, Luyia, and Nandi) are found next to each other along the equator. The majority of the people speak Bantu languages but in the north of Uganda and down the Great Rift Valley in Kenya and Tanzania people speak Sudanic languages. In Kenya's northeast are nomadic Somali-speaking peoples (see pages 38–39).

SURVIVAL OF TRADITIONAL WAYS

Ways of life change with the varied climatic conditions. There are nomadic herders and cattle-keepers. The majority are farmers growing maize, millet, and vegetables, who keep some cattle, sheep, and goats. Cash crops like tea, coffee, and cotton are grown with success on peasant smallholdings. Social groupings range from small bands of herders to farmers like the Kikuyu in Kenya who have elders, and kingdoms that have hereditary chiefs and royal families, like the Ganda of Uganda with their ruler the Kabaka.

To the west and southwest of Lake Victoria in present-day Uganda and Tanzania are a group of traditional kingdoms – Buganda, Toro, Bunyoro, Buhaya, and others. The peoples of this area eat bananas and plantains, rather than maize, as their main food.

Kenya, where during the colonial period there were many white settler-farmers, inherited a particularly good road–rail system, which has continued to aid its relatively prosperous development. Economic growth in Uganda and Tanzania has been limited by the problems faced by these countries. Civil war took place in Uganda in the 1970s, and in Tanzania frequent drought and long distances have resulted in poor communications.

Left Zanzibar, "the clove island," was the 19th-century traveler's doorway into East Africa. In 1829 the Sultan of Oman transferred his capital here. It contained the main slave market. Its long Middle East connections show in the tall houses along narrow streets, with balconies from which secluded Muslim women can peep out.

East Africa since 1945

1945 Britain is the main colonial power in the area.
1952–56: Kenya Mau-Mau uprising. Inter-tribal tension and resentment against European settlers causes violence.
1961: Tanzania Tanganyika, led by Dr Julius Nyerere, becomes independent: joins with island of Zanzibar in 1964 to become Tanzania.
1962: Uganda Gains independence from Britain. Kabaka (King) of Buganda becomes head of state. **Burundi and Rwanda** These two small inland states gain independence.
1963: Kenya Gains independence from Britain.
1966: Uganda Constitution suspended. Prime Minister Obote overthrows Kabaka and ends role of kingdoms.
1967: Tanzania Nyerere issues his Arusha Declaration in which he sets out his aim for Tanzanian development and self-reliance.
1971: Uganda Obote overthrown by Army leader, General Idi Amin.
1971–79: Uganda Amin rules Uganda through a reign of terror: up to 300,000 Ugandans killed by his secret police.
1972–73: Burundi Violence between Hutu and Tutsi peoples kills thousands. Order restored. Burundi then develops close economic links with Rwanda and the Democratic Republic of Congo.
1972: Kenya Failed coup attempt.
1978: Kenya Arap Moi becomes president.
1979: Uganda Amin overthrown after his invasion of Tanzania fails.
1980: Uganda Obote re-elected as president but civil war continues for four years in wake of Amin's brutality.
1994: Rwanda An estimated 200,000–500,000 civilians, most of them from the minority Tutsi group, murdered by Hutu militias.

Right Much of East Africa lies between 3,300ft and 6,600ft above sea level. There are several areas of mountainous country, and this region contains the two highest peaks in Africa: Mt Kilimanjaro (19,341ft) and Mt Kenya (17,061ft). Both are volcanoes. The Great Rift Valley (see page 10) stretches from Kenya into Tanzania, and contains several lakes, some of them salty (Lake Natron).

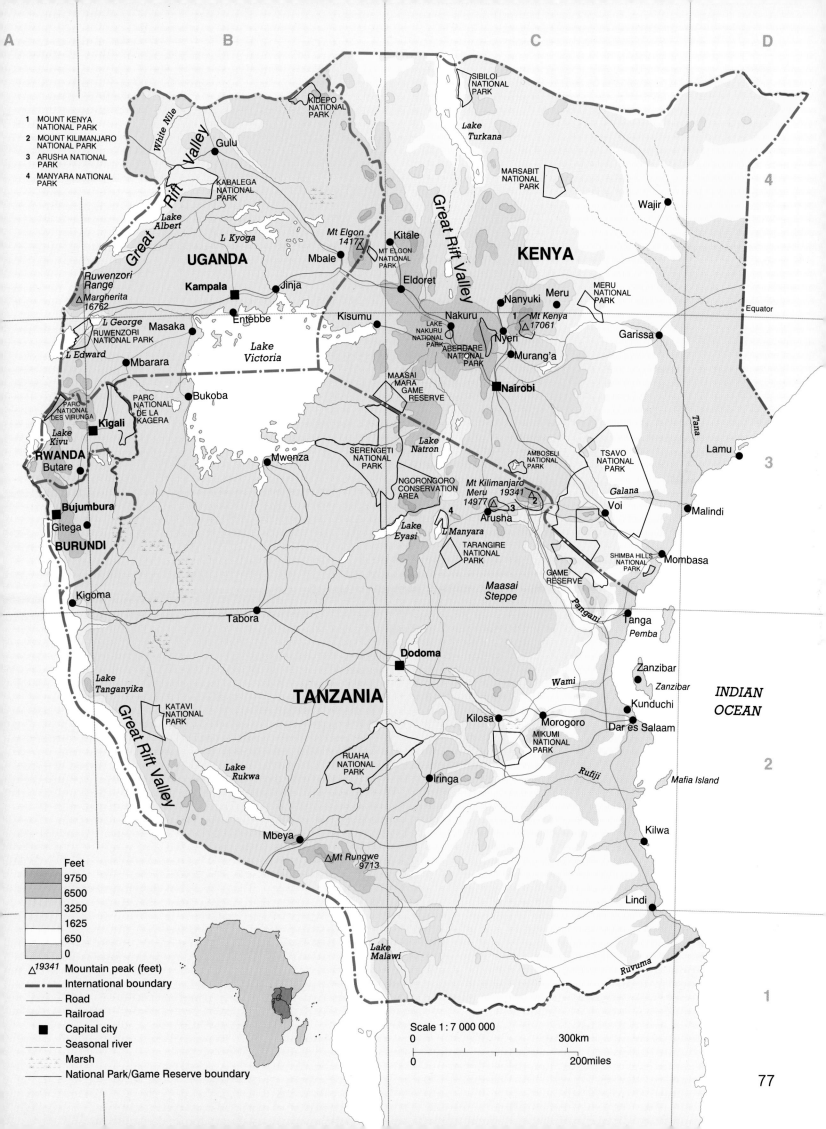

A   B   C   D

1 MOUNT KENYA
NATIONAL PARK
2 MOUNT KILIMANJARO
NATIONAL PARK
3 ARUSHA NATIONAL
PARK
4 MANYARA NATIONAL
PARK

White Nile

Great Rift Valley

Gulu

KIDEPO
NATIONAL
PARK

SIBILOI
NATIONAL
PARK

*Lake
Turkana*

KABALEGA
NATIONAL
PARK

*Lake
Albert*

L Kyoga

Mt Elgon
1417△
Kitale

MT ELGON
NATIONAL
PARK

Mbale

Eldoret

Great Rift Valley

MARSABIT
NATIONAL
PARK

Wajir

KENYA

UGANDA

Ruwenzori
Range

△ Margherita
16762

Kampala ■

Jinja

Nanyuki

Meru

MERU
NATIONAL
PARK

L George

Masaka

Entebbe

Kisumu

Nakuru

LAKE
NAKURU
NATIONAL
PARK

1 △ Mt Kenya
17061

RUWENZORI
NATIONAL PARK

L Edward

Mbarara

*Lake
Victoria*

Nyeri

Garissa

Equator

ABERDARE
NATIONAL
PARK

Murang'a

PARC
NATIONAL
DES VIRUNGA

PARC
NATIONAL
DE LA
KAGERA

Bukoba

■ **Nairobi**

Tana

Kigali ■

*Lake
Kivu*

MAASAI
MARA
GAME
RESERVE

Lamu

RWANDA

Butare

Mwenza

SERENGETI
NATIONAL
PARK

*Lake
Natron*

AMBOSELI
NATIONAL
PARK

TSAVO
NATIONAL
PARK

Bujumbura ■

Gitega

NGORONGORO
CONSERVATION
AREA

Mt Kilimanjaro
19341
Meru
14977

2 △

Galana

Voi

Malindi

BURUNDI

4

*Lake
Eyasi*

3 △

Arusha

L Manyara

TARANGIRE
NATIONAL
PARK

SHIMBA HILLS
NATIONAL
PARK

Mombasa

Kigoma

*Maasai
Steppe*

GAME
RESERVE

Tabora

Pangani

Tanga

Pemba

Dodoma ■

Wami

Zanzibar

Zanzibar

*Lake
Tanganyika*

TANZANIA

Kilosa

Morogoro

Kunduchi

Dar es Salaam

**INDIAN
OCEAN**

KATAVI
NATIONAL
PARK

MIKUMI
NATIONAL
PARK

Rufiji

Mafia Island

RUAHA
NATIONAL
PARK

*Lake
Rukwa*

Iringa

Great Rift Valley

Kilwa

Mbeya

△ Mt Rungwe
9713

Feet

9750
6500
3250
1625
650
0

Lindi

△ 19341   Mountain peak (feet)
⋅—⋅—⋅   International boundary
  Road
  Railroad
■   Capital city
– – –   Seasonal river
  Marsh
  National Park/Game Reserve boundary

*Lake
Malawi*

Ruvuma

Scale 1 : 7 000 000

0   300km

0   200miles

4

3

2

1

77

THE GAME PARKS OF EAST AFRICA

T HE REMOVAL OF TROPICAL FORESTS AND the spread of agriculture, together with erosion caused by overgrazing of cattle, has caused the loss of much of the habitat of African wildlife. It decreased sharply in the 20th century. Nevertheless, Africa remains the home of many of the world's more spectacular species. This is largely due to the great parks which have existed for almost a century (see map page 77).

The parks' function has changed greatly in recent years. Originally they were established to shelter and protect wildlife from people – from big game hunting for sport as much as from the local population who then lost their supplies of "bushmeat." But the removal of humans as predators has sometimes meant an increase in the number of certain species which has upset the natural balance.

CHANGE IN THE USE OF GAME PARKS

Increasingly game parks are being seen not as areas that should be sealed off from all outside influences, but as areas to be used and managed like any other part of the country. For example, it is now understood that a mixed wildlife population

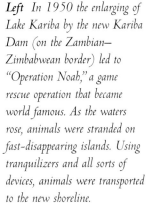

Left Since firearms are available and there has been a ready market for (sometimes illegal) wildlife products, poaching has remained a problem, and has led to violence against tourists as well. Elephant and rhino are the main targets. Those who actually do the killing are one small factor in the chain of people receiving profit from the trade.

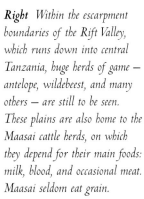

Left In 1950 the enlarging of Lake Kariba by the new Kariba Dam (on the Zambian–Zimbabwean border) led to "Operation Noah," a game rescue operation that became world famous. As the waters rose, animals were stranded on fast-disappearing islands. Using tranquilizers and all sorts of devices, animals were transported to the new shoreline.

Right Within the escarpment boundaries of the Rift Valley, which runs down into central Tanzania, huge herds of game — antelope, wildebeest, and many others — are still to be seen. These plains are also home to the Maasai cattle herds, on which they depend for their main foods: milk, blood, and occasional meat. Maasai seldom eat grain.

Above A Maasai family in their homestead of low-built mud-and-stick houses. Their dress, which used to be made of leather, is now reddish-tan cloth – the color of leather. Maasai herdsmen now share the plains with game and with tourists. Traditionally the men and boys move with the herds, leaving the women and young children at home.

uses the vegetable resources available more efficiently than one species. Therefore, culling wildlife may produce more animal protein for the local human population than using the same land for a cattle ranch.

Game parks play an increasing part in the national economy through tourism, and they may also be used for controlled fishing, limited grazing, and planning new forests.

GAME PARKS AND THE MAASAI

The existence of game parks still raises great problems for people like the Maasai. Their traditional way of life, with their hunting and their cattle-keeping, covered the same areas as the parks in Kenya.

The Maasai now have some permanent water supplies, and some of them have settled on small ranches round the fringes of the national parks. A large number of Maasai men find compatible work as game scouts. But they no longer have the freedom to roam with their cattle wherever they wish, nor to hunt wild animals. There is a danger that modern tourism will turn the Maasai into a mere spectacle.

S.E. Central Africa

Malawi, Zambia, and Zimbabwe (formerly Nyasaland, Northern Rhodesia, and Southern Rhodesia) were for a short time united in the Central African Federation, a British colony. Zimbabwe has had a troubled history as a former British colony where self-government was granted to the white minority. After a bitter civil war between white settlers and African nationalists it became independent under black majority rule in 1980. A legacy of colonial rule has recently brought renewed instability.

The fourth nation in southeast central Africa, the former Portuguese colony of Mozambique, also had a period of troubles leading up to its independence in 1975. Throughout these four countries almost all the African peoples speak one or other of the Bantu languages, and share rather similar ways of life. There are Muslims along the coast and in some inland regions, but in general the people still follow traditional religions or are Christians. Apart from some large organized chiefdoms (such as Barotseland), most communities were small and directed by headmen.

Cash crops such as tobacco, tea, coffee, cotton, and rice are important. In northern Zambia there is wealth from the mining of minerals in the Copper Belt (see pages 84–85). With the availability of hydroelectric power from river dams, the whole region, given political stability, may look to a prosperous future.

Left *The Victoria Falls, on the Zambezi river which lies between Zambia and Zimbabwe, plunge 330ft into a narrow (100ft) chasm. They were named by the English explorer, David Livingstone. Their African name is Mosu-oa-tun-ya, "smoke that thunders."*

Southeast central Africa since 1945

1953: Creation of Federation of Rhodesia and Nyasaland – a self-governing colony dominated by white settlers in Rhodesia.

1964: Zambia, Malawi Zambia (formerly Northern Rhodesia) and Malawi (formerly Nyasaland) independent after break-up of Federation in 1963. **Mozambique** War breaks out between white settlers backed by Portuguese army and black nationalist movements.

1965: Southern Rhodesia Declares its independence from Britain. A white-dominated country led by Ian Smith.

1972–79: Southern Rhodesia Civil war develops between settlers and black nationalist movements based in neighboring countries.

1974: Mozambique Portuguese resistance collapses – leads to revolution in Portugal itself.

1975: Mozambique Independence. **Zambia** Railway to Tanzania's coast, built with Chinese funds, is completed.

1979: Southern Rhodesia (Zimbabwe) Lancaster House agreement ends Rhodesian civil war. Power to be handed over to black majority after elections.

1980: Zimbabwe Robert Mugabe elected as Prime Minister of Zimbabwe.

2001: Zimbabwe Mugabe re-elected to power but accused of rigging the results. Seizures of white-owned land leads to economic crisis and an estimated 5 million people in need of aid.

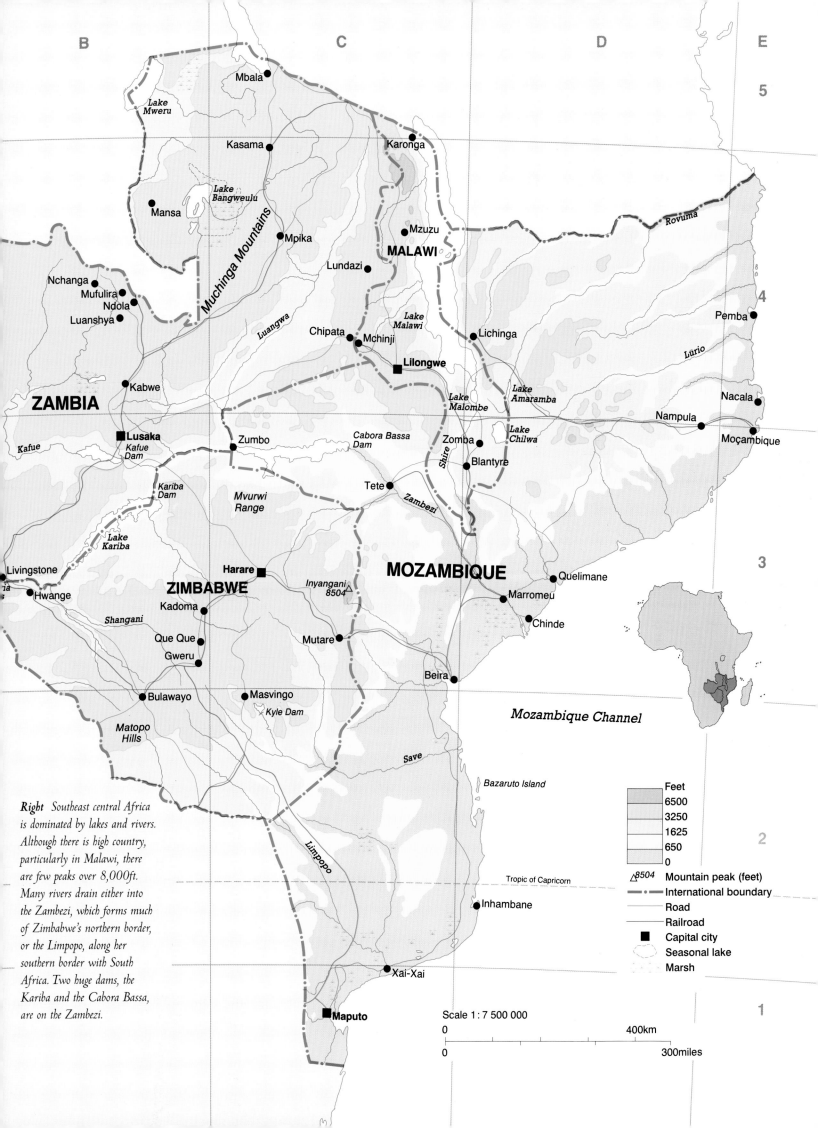

B · · · C · · · D · · · E

5

Mbala

Lake
Mweru

Kasama   Karonga

Lake
Bangweulu

Mansa   Mzuzu

Mpika   MALAWI

Nchanga   Lundazi
Mufulira
Ndola   Lake
Luanshya   Malawi

ZAMBIA   Chipata   Mchinji   Lichinga   4

Kabwe   ■ Lilongwe

Lake   Lake
Malombe   Amaramba   Nacala

Lusaka   Lake
Kafue   ■Lusaka   Chilwa   Nampula
Kafue   Zomba   Moçambique
Dam   Zumbo   Cabora Bassa   Blantyre
Kariba   Dam
Dam   Shire
Mvurwi   Tete
Range   Zambezi

Lake
Kariba   Quelimane   3

Livingstone   Inyangani   MOZAMBIQUE   Marromeu
Hwange   ZIMBABWE ■Harare   8504△
Chinde
Shangani   Kadoma

Que Que   Mutare
Gweru

Beira

Bulawayo   Masvingo

Matopo   Kyle Dam
Hills

Mozambique Channel

Save

Bazaruto Island

                                                    Feet
                                                    6500
Right Southeast central Africa   3250
is dominated by lakes and rivers.   1625
Although there is high country,   650
particularly in Malawi, there   0
are few peaks over 8,000ft.
Many rivers drain either into   Tropic of Capricorn   △8504 Mountain peak (feet)
the Zambezi, which forms much   ·–·– International boundary
of Zimbabwe's northern border,   Inhambane   Road
or the Limpopo, along her   Railroad
southern border with South   ■ Capital city
Africa. Two huge dams, the   Limpopo   Seasonal lake
Kariba and the Cabora Bassa,   Xai-Xai   Marsh
are on the Zambezi.

                    ■ Maputo   Scale 1 : 7 500 000   1

                              0   400km

                              0   300miles

ZIMBABWE

"ZIMBABWE," IN THE LANGUAGE OF THE local Shona people, means "house of the Chief." It refers to a large number of stone-walled enclosures that are found on the plateaus and hills of south central Zimbabwe. This country, formerly Southern Rhodesia (see pages 80–81), now takes its name from them. The largest and most spectacular of these remains is known as Great Zimbabwe.

THE HISTORY OF GREAT ZIMBABWE

The enclosures are in an area rich in gold and other metals. It seems that as early as 650 CE a centralized state began to develop. Its ruler was known as the Monomutapa, and it prospered by raising crops and cattle. Later, the Shona became skilled miners and metalworkers, and sold much gold, copper, and ivory to Indian Ocean traders.

Great Zimbabwe was most probably the Monomutapa's capital, and the center of the religious life of his people. It was built over a period of perhaps 400 years, but during the 16th century, for reasons that are not clear, the ruler and his court left Great Zimbabwe.

WESTERN TRAVELERS VISIT

Portuguese traders and soldiers wrote about the great stone ruins, and a German explorer, Karl Mauch, visited them in 1871. He camped nearby for some months, and became convinced that only outsiders, not the ancestors of the local Shona people, could have built such impressive walls.

In 1891 Cecil Rhodes, the South African politician and imperialist, sent an English traveler, J.T. Bent, to study the ruins, and he also concluded that the builders had come from outside, and were perhaps Phoenicians. White settlers in Rhodesia accepted this idea. They dug among the ruins for treasure and took away objects they found there. An Ancient Ruins Company was formed by Europeans to sell their plunder and a great deal of damage was caused to the site.

Right This is how part of the king's residence would have looked in the 1400s (in the photo of the ruins opposite it is the large circle at the top). Near the Conical Tower — probably a store for grain — the buttressed walls (16ft thick at their base) were decorated with a chevron (zigzag) pattern. The outer wall was 825ft long and 32ft in height. The expertly cut and laid stones (no mortar was used) showed the skill of the builders.

Great Zimbabwe

THE SHONA RECEIVE RECOGNITION

In 1905, however, and again in 1929, professional archeologists who had excavated in the Middle East came to work in Southern Rhodesia. The earlier group looked first at the smaller *zimbabwe* before beginning their work at Great Zimbabwe.

Both groups came to one conclusion – that there was no reason at all to think that Arabs or Phoenicians were the builders of the great stone enclosures, and every reason to think that it was the work of the same Shona people who still lived there. The Arab and Chinese pots and plates (some of it porcelain of the Ming period) that were found would have been goods obtained through trade with the coast some 380mi away. It is not coincidence that Great Zimbabwe was built on a trade route to the coast.

Below Most of the ruins are walls of circular or oval enclosures, which seem never to have had roofs. Large boulders were incorporated in the walls. Smaller enclosures were probably for cattle, built next to thatched houses made of earth and poles.

MINERAL RESOURCES

ALMOST ALL AFRICAN NATIONS HAVE SOME mineral resources; many are exceedingly rich in either variety or quantity. Morocco has over half the world's reserves of phosphate; the Democratic Republic of Congo, best known for copper, leads in world production of industrial diamonds and of cobalt; Gabon has particularly large deposits of iron ore; Sierra Leone is famous for its diamonds.

Uranium, now so valuable, is found in over a dozen African countries but is largely unexploited. Bauxite is widely found in West Africa. Diamonds are the most widely found gemstone; others are amethysts, rubies, garnets, and emeralds. In 1967 a new gemstone was discovered in northeast Tanzania, which has been given the name Tanzanite. It is found in several colors, which when treated with heat turn blue, the type usually marketed.

Mineral wealth has not always in the past been an advantage to African nations. Often very little of the wealth stayed in the country and extraction led to social problems for the workers. Now, with nations independent, there is hope that rich deposits may be exploited well, bringing wealth within Africa.

EXPLOITING THE MINERAL RESERVES

The extraction, processing, and transportation of minerals is costly. When deposits are discovered far inland, in under-populated areas with demanding climates, it is not surprising that many of them remain "unexploited." The areas that have been exploited have both great quantities of minerals and access to Western money and technology. These are, particularly, the Copper Belt of Zambia and the Democratic Republic of Congo; the diamond mines of Tanzania; and South Africa's great deposits of gold, on the ridge of rock, the Rand, and diamonds around the town of Kimberley.

IMPORTING LABOR

Most mineral extraction requires a large labor force, as well as technology. The towns and cities of the Copper Belt and the Rand have been known for their vast number of migrant laborers – African men who leave their homes and families in rural areas, sometimes in another country, and work for a contracted period in the mines. They must live in bleak prison-like hostels, sending money to support their families. A small landlocked country like

Above Open-cast copper mining at Likasi, Democratic Republic of Congo. In this country a state-owned organization controls mining and refining, although experts from overseas are still employed.

Left Mufulira, one of a cluster of eight mining townships on the Zambian Copper Belt. These towns make extensive use of poor agricultural land for housing.

Left Stacking paper-thin copper sheets for export. The copper is refined so that its value in relation to its bulk is high. Because Zambia is a landlocked country, the cost of transportation adds greatly to the price of its raw materials.

Right Two large steam trains meet on the main railway link between Bloemfontein and Bethlehem in South Africa. New capital investment will eventually lead to the replacement of all steam trains in South Africa.

Above Underground mining in the Democratic Republic of Congo. Both open-cast and underground methods are used.

Below Many diamonds come from long-extinct volcanoes. Rock is drilled and then crushed to release the diamonds.

Lesotho might have one in eight of its male adult population absent at the mines, and the money they send home is a large part of the national income.

THE COPPER BELT

Africa is a major producer of the world's copper, and there are copper deposits in many of its countries. The copper-mining industry in Zambia is centered around a number of mining towns (Kitwe-Nkana, Ndola, Nchanga, and others) in what is known as the Copper Belt. Copper was first mined in precolonial times, and a modern copper industry developed in the mid-1920s. Most of Zambia's export earnings come from copper.

SOUTHERN AFRICA

ALTHOUGH THE COUNTRIES OF THIS REGION have their own governments, they are very much dominated by South Africa. Lesotho, Swaziland, and Botswana once came under direct British rule; Namibia (former German South West Africa) became a South African trust territory. It finally became an independent nation state in March 1990.

All the Africans of these five nations speak Bantu languages with the exception of the Khoisan peoples of the central and southwest deserts. The Khoikhoi, of whom few are left, were cattle herders; the San and other groups were hunter-gatherers (see pages 88–89).

The first white settlers, in the early 17th century, were Dutch and they were joined by French and British settlers in the 18th and 19th centuries. The Dutch farmers, in their search for good land, came into conflict with Bantu-speaking peoples who already used the same type of land (see pages 26–27).

The discovery of gold and diamonds on the Rand (near Johannesburg) was one factor in the Anglo–Boer War of 1899–1902, a cause of continuing bitterness between the Afrikaners and the English-speaking whites. The mines use black African migrant labor from other states and South Africa's neighbors are therefore kept economically dependent. When self-government was granted in 1910 the majority blacks and Indians (who had been encouraged to settle to provide another labor force) were excluded from any part in government. Their exclusion, and that of people of mixed race, was the basis of apartheid, which was finally removed in the early 1990s.

Right From a narrow coastal plain, the land gradually climbs to the high veld then descends to the drier lands of the Kalahari Desert. The highest land is in the landlocked kingdom of Lesotho, with mountains over 10,000ft. More fertile land lies in the east and extreme south.

Southern Africa since 1945

1948: South Africa National Party comes to power. Represents white-dominated "Afrikaner" viewpoint.
1960: South Africa Massacre of black demonstrators at Sharpeville.
1961: South Africa Leaves Commonwealth and becomes a republic. Continues policy of apartheid ("separate development of races").
1963: South Africa Nelson Mandela, leader of the African National Congress (ANC), is imprisoned.
1966: Botswana Gains independence from Britain.
1976: Transkei, the first black "homeland" gains "independence" but dependent on South Africa.
1978: South Africa P.W. Botha succeeds Dr Vorster as South African leader.
1985: South Africa State of Emergency declared by Government; more restrictions on press freedom.
1989: South Africa Dr Botha resigns. Succeeded by more liberal F.W. de Klerk.
1990: South Africa Nelson Mandela released.
Namibia Becomes independent after years of South African control.
1994: South Africa First multiracial general election, with the ANC winning a large majority.
2001: South Africa It is predicted that within a few years AIDS will reduce life expectancy for black people in South Africa from 60 to 40 years.

Left Women of the Herero people, who live in western Botswana and in Namibia, still wear turbans and long cotton dresses made in the style introduced by the 19th century missionaries of the (German) Rhenish Missionary Society (see pages 30–31). The Herero are still active Lutherans, and their church has been involved in Namibia's long struggle for the right to gain independence from South Africa.

A

Etosha Pan

Ugab

NAMIBIA

ATLANTIC OCEAN

Swakopmund

Windho[e]

Walvis Bay

Namib Desert

Lüderitz

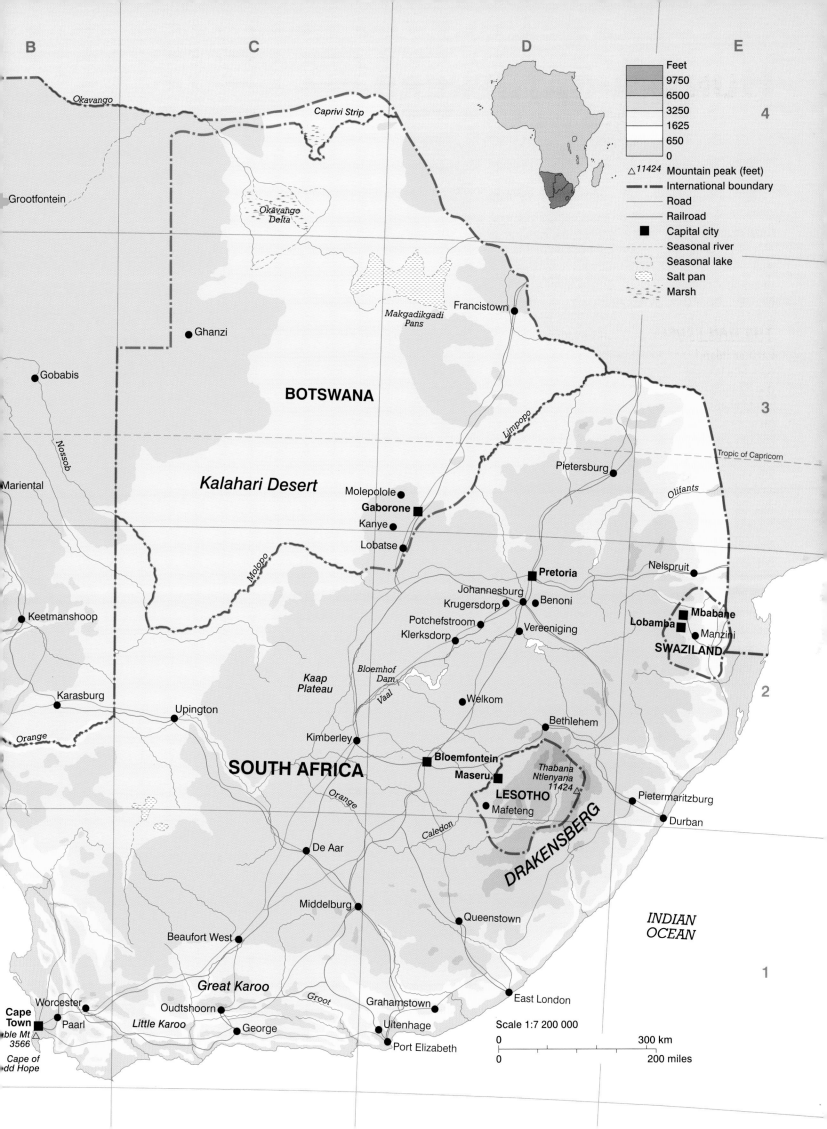

B **C** **D** **E**

4

Okavango

Caprivi Strip

Grootfontein

Feet
9750
6500
3250
1625
650
0

△11424 Mountain peak (feet)
International boundary
Road
Railroad
Capital city
Seasonal river
Seasonal lake
Salt pan
Marsh

Okavango Delta

Gobabis

• Ghanzi

Makgadikgadi Pans

Francistown

3

BOTSWANA

Nossob

Mariental

Kalahari Desert

Pietersburg

Tropic of Capricorn

Olifants

Molepolole •

Gaborone ■

Limpopo

Kanye •

Lobatse •

Nelspruit •

Keetmanshoop •

Pretoria ■

Johannesburg •
Krugersdorp • • Benoni
Potchefstroom •
Klerksdorp • • Vereeniging

Lobamba ■ **Mbabane**
Lobamba
Manzini •

SWAZILAND

Molopo

2

Bloemhof Dam

Karasburg •

Kaap Plateau

Vaal

Welkom •

Upington •

Orange

Bethlehem •

Kimberley •

SOUTH AFRICA

Bloemfontein ■
Maseru ■

Thabana Ntlenyana 11424 △

Pietermaritzburg •

Orange

LESOTHO

Durban •

Mafeteng •

Caledon

DRAKENSBERG

De Aar •

Middelburg •

Queenstown •

INDIAN OCEAN

1

Beaufort West •

Great Karoo

Worcester •

Groot

Grahamstown •

East London •

Cape **Town** ■
ble Mt 3566 △
• Paarl

Oudtshoorn •

Little Karoo

George •

Uitenhage •

Scale 1:7 200 000

0 _____ 300 km

0 _____ 200 miles

Cape of dd Hope

Port Elizabeth

HUNTER-GATHERERS

THE PEOPLE WHO WERE LIVING AT THE TIP of South Africa when the first European explorers arrived were quite unlike the West Africans. They had yellowish skins, and were cattle-herders, not farmers. The Dutch called them *Hottentots* (Dutch for "stutterer," because of the click sound in their speech) but they called themselves *Khoikhoin*, "Men of men," and it is as Khoikhoi that they are known today.

THE SAN PEOPLE

Farther inland were much shorter yellow-skinned people who spoke languages of the same family as the Khoikhoi – click languages. The Khoikhoi called them San. These people, once known as Bushmen, did not plant crops or keep cattle, but hunted game and gathered wild honey, wild fruit, and roots. Otherwise, they were much like the Khoikhoi.

Over the years the San have been pushed back into the drier country where cattle and crops do not flourish. Now most San people live in and around the Kalahari Desert in the northwest of South Africa, Namibia, and Botswana. They still try to follow the old way of life, living in small bands, without houses or shelter except bushes, finding what they want on the veld. During the dry season,

the San are expert at finding roots and melon fruit which provide them with liquid as well as food.

Meat is provided from the game that the men bring back from hunting, using bow and poisoned arrows. Use will be made of almost every part of the animal, skin, and bones as well. Some men work on the farms of whites or Bantu-speaking Africans and have money to buy iron knives, cotton cloth, and tobacco.

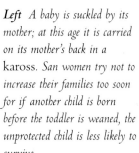

Left A baby is suckled by its mother; at this age it is carried on its mother's back in a kaross. San women try not to increase their families too soon for if another child is born before the toddler is weaned, the unprotected child is less likely to survive.

Left The San way of life relates back to the Stone Age. The semidesert land to which they have gradually been confined is becoming more barren every year. Drought and over-grazing by stock belonging to settled Africans extends the desert, and has led to attempts to settle the San people.

Right A small band of San people gathering food as they move across the veld. They are picking spiny jelly melons. Some are holding digging sticks which they use to get at juicy roots. Others carry bundles that contain their few possessions – mainly large gourds and water containers made from ostrich eggs.

AFRICA IN THE WORLD

SINCE THE 1950S THE COUNTRIES OF AFRICA have become independent nations. Many of the problems that the new states had to face were the result of the colonial division of Africa. Boundary lines were drawn on maps that had no connection with the people who lived in the land, especially where people were used to a nomadic or semi-nomadic life. Now, however, Africa's nations are all aligned in various political and economic groupings, some of them international. All of them now belong to the United Nations Organization.

MEMBERSHIP OF ORGANIZATIONS

Morocco excepted, all African countries are members of the African Union (AU). Replacing the Organization of African Unity (OAU) in 2002, the new African Union is loosely modeled

Left Sugar forms about 90 percent of Mauritius' exports. The settlers who came to the island were African slaves, Arab sailors, Chinese laborers, Indian traders, plus French and British.

Above The local people fish in the shallow waters off Zanzibar. The island used to be the Western travelers' doorway to the continent but today it is economically and politically separate from it.

on that of the European Union (EU), and has amongst its aims security, stability, development and cooperation within Africa.

The Arab League is "a voluntary organization of sovereign Arab states" which was founded in 1945 to encourage economic, cultural and social cooperation between Arab countries. Ten of the 22 members are African, with the remaining 12 being found in the Middle East. The African members of the League form an important bridge between the nations of Black Africa and those of the Arab world.

The Economic Commission for Africa (ECA), which has its headquarters in Addis Ababa, Ethiopia, aims to promote international cooperation for African development, and to

support the social and economic growth of its members.

The Cotonou Agreement is another grouping that is important for the economic future of Africa. It provides the structure for trade and cooperation between the European Union (EU) and over 70 member states from Africa, the Caribbean and the Pacific.

African nations also participate in and benefit from the various United Nations agencies. UNESCO (United Nations Educational, Scientific, and Cultural Organization), for instance, has regional headquarters in Dakar, Senegal, Cairo, Egypt and Nairobi, Kenya. The International Labor Organization (ILO) has its regional office in Addis Ababa, Ethiopia.

Below The sunny beaches of the East African coast are now havens for tourists from all over the world.

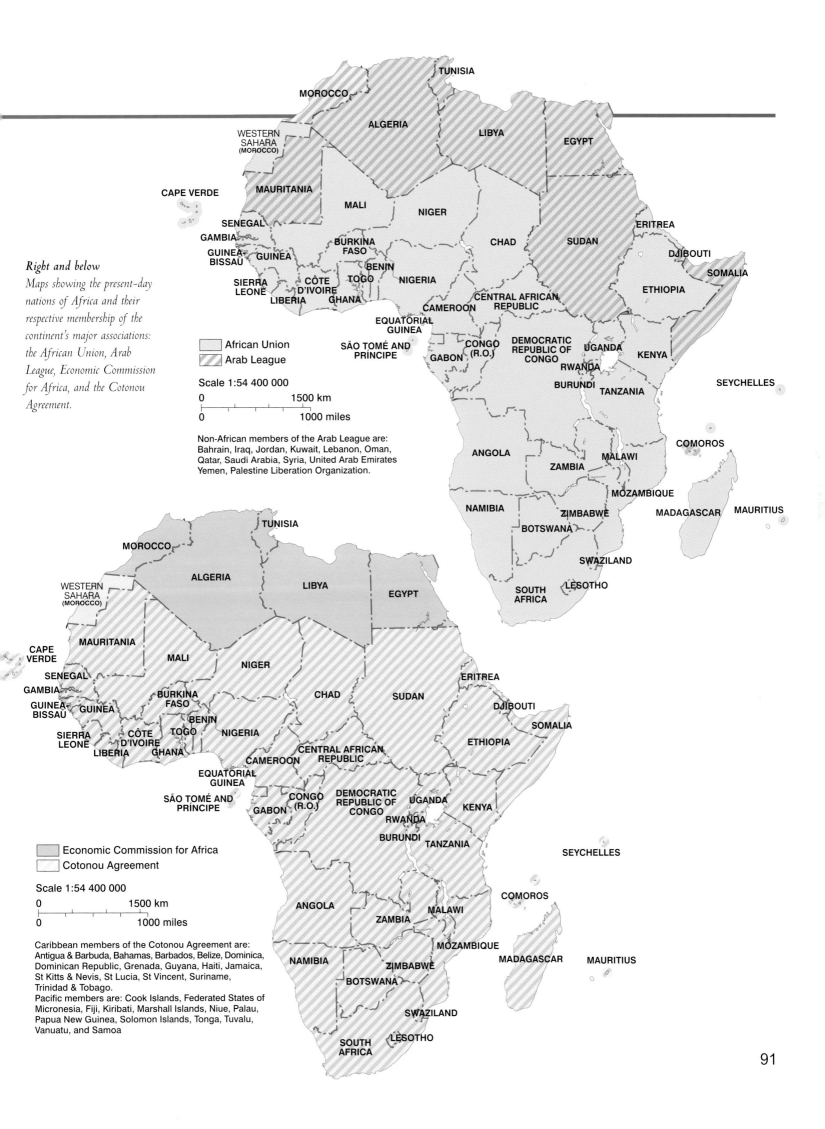

Right and below

Maps showing the present-day nations of Africa and their respective membership of the continent's major associations: the African Union, Arab League, Economic Commission for Africa, and the Cotonou Agreement.

■ African Union
▨ Arab League

Scale 1:54 400 000

0 — 1500 km
0 — 1000 miles

Non-African members of the Arab League are:
Bahrain, Iraq, Jordan, Kuwait, Lebanon, Oman, Qatar, Saudi Arabia, Syria, United Arab Emirates Yemen, Palestine Liberation Organization.

▨ Economic Commission for Africa
▨ Cotonou Agreement

Scale 1:54 400 000

0 — 1500 km
0 — 1000 miles

Caribbean members of the Cotonou Agreement are:
Antigua & Barbuda, Bahamas, Barbados, Belize, Dominica, Dominican Republic, Grenada, Guyana, Haiti, Jamaica, St Kitts & Nevis, St Lucia, St Vincent, Suriname, Trinidad & Tobago.
Pacific members are: Cook Islands, Federated States of Micronesia, Fiji, Kiribati, Marshall Islands, Niue, Palau, Papua New Guinea, Solomon Islands, Tonga, Tuvalu, Vanuatu, and Samoa

Glossary

alpine plant Plant growing on mountains above the timberline.

broad-leaved forest Evergreen forest of trees with wide leaves (i.e., not conifers).

bronze An alloy (mixture) of copper and tin (and sometimes other elements). In history, Bronze Age cultures date from about 4000 to 1600 BCE.

citadel A fortress commanding a city; a stronghold.

clan An extended family or group of families descended from the same pair of ancestors.

continental plate Section of Pangea, a vast single landmass that existed 200 million years ago. It separated into sections or plates that form the modern continents.

delta The mouth of a river, built up with alluvial deposits (sand, mud, and silt) into a triangular shape, like a Greek capital D, "delta" (Δ).

dhow (Arabic) Sailing boat with a high poop, now used as a general term for many types of boats that used the monsoon winds to sail from the Indian sub-continent or Arabian peninsula to East African coastal ports.

diviner Religious official (often a priest) who interprets present happenings (illnesses and so on), and foretells the future by looking at signs (such as the way stones or nuts fall on a special tray).

eland (Afrikaans) Large African antelope with short spirally twisted horns in, unusually, both males and females.

fault A break, or area of fracture, usually with reference to a layer of rock. Movements of adjacent rock occur around such breaks and a number of them form a fault system.

fossil Remains (bone, wood, and so on) of animals, vegetables, humans, preserved in earth or rock, usually for very long periods.

French Foreign Legion Several companies of non-French soldiers but with French officers and sergeants mainly serving in overseas French colonies, especially in North Africa (Morocco, Tunisia, Algeria).

hinterland Region beyond a coast, often linked to the coast in providing supplies.

Iron Age Period of human culture when people learned to smelt iron and to make and use iron tools. It dates from about 1600 to 1000 BCE.

Islam The religion founded in the Arabian peninsula by the prophet Muhammad in the early 7th century CE. It declares that there is no god but Allah and that Muhammad is the Messenger of Allah. Its holy book is the Koran and its followers are known as Muslims.

lichen Any one of a number of plants made up of the association of algae and fungi. Lichens grow on a solid surface, such as a rock.

mandate Territory (in this book refers to a former German colony) entrusted by one power to another (here the League of Nations and a member nation) to govern responsibly.

metal-casting Giving shape to a substance by pouring molten metal into a form or mold.

missionary Person sent on a special service or mission; used of religious preachers/teachers sent by one church to preach and teach in another country.

Muslim A person who follows the Islamic religion.

oracle Wise message about the future given by a diviner such as a priest or god.

protectorate Territory (often conquered) ruled by one power at the request of another. The term was used after the Second World War of former German and Italian colonies, some of which were previously known as mandates.

rift system A series of fault lines which have resulted in long breaks in the Earth's crust, with very high and abrupt drops to valley floors. Many are on the ocean floors, but the African rift system, one of the largest in the world, runs from the Red Sea to southern Africa.

savanna (Spanish) Treeless plain. The term was originally used in tropical America but now usually refers to the vast open grasslands of East Africa.

shantytown A poor and depressed area with inadequate housing.

Stone Age First known period of human culture, when stone tools were used. It dates from about 10,000 to 4000 BCE.

UNESCO Abbreviation of United Nations Educational, Scientific and Cultural Organization.

veld (Dutch) Wild grassland with scattered trees, especially in southern Africa.

FURTHER READING

Books for adults
Kwame Anthony Appiah, Henry Louis, Jr. Gates *Africana: The Encyclopedia of the African and African American Experience* (Basic Civitas Books), 1999.
Guy Arnold, *The New South Africa* (Macmillan), 2000.
Carol Beckwith, Angela Fisher, Graham Hancock, *African Ark: People and Ancient Cultures of Ethiopia and the Horn of Africa* (Harry N. Abrams), 1990.
Rodney Davenport and Christopher Saunders, *South Africa* (Macmillan), 2000.
Basil Davidson, *Africa in History: Themes and Outlines* (Scribner), 1995.
Basil Davidson, *Modern Africa. A social and political history*, 3rd edition (Addison & Wesley), 1995.
John Iliffe, *Africans: The History of a Continent* (Cambridge University Press), 1996.
Robert William July, *A History of the African People* (Waveland Press), 1997.
Richard Pankhurst, *The Ethiopians: A History* (Blackwell), 2001.

Books for young people
Jamie Hetfield, Marianne Johnson, *The Maasai of East Africa* (Powerkids), 1997.
Francesca Lyman, *Inside the Dzanga-Sangha Rain Forest: Exploring the Heart of Central Africa* (Workman Publishing), 1998.
Garrett Nagle, *Country Studies: South Africa* (Heinemann Library), 1999.
Sean Sheehan, *Great African Kingdoms* (Raintree/Steck Vaughn), 1998.
Sean Sheehan, *South Africa Since Apartheid* (Hodder Wayland), 2002.
Velma Maia Thomas, *Lest We Forget: The Passage from Africa to Slavery and Emancipation* (Crown Pub), 1997.

GAZETTEER

The gazetteer lists places and features, such as islands or rivers, found on the maps. Each has a separate entry including a page and grid reference number. For example: Aswan 53 J2

All features are shown in *italic* type. For example:
Atbara, r. 11 F6, 73 D5

A letter after the feature describes the kind of feature:
i. island; *isls.* islands; *r.* river
mt. mountain; *mts.* mountains;

Abaya, *Lake* 73 D3
Abbe, *Lake* 73 E4
Abéché 68 C6
Abeokuta 59 E2
Abidjan 11 B5, 59 D2
Abuja 11 C5, 59 F2
Accra 11 B5, 59 D2
Adamawa Highlands 59 G2
Addis Ababa 11 F5, 73 D2
Aden, Gulf of 11 G6, 73 F4
Adigrat 73 D4
Agades 59 F4
Air, mts. 11 C6, 59 F4
Akosombo Dam 59 E2
Albert, Lake 11 F5, 68 E4, 77 B4
Alexandria 53 I3
Algiers 11 C8, 52 E4
Al Jawf 53 H2
Amaramba, Lake 81 D4
Annaba 52 F4
Antananarivo 11 G3
Arabian Desert 11 F7, 53 J2
Arusha 77 C3
Asmara 11 F6, 73 D5
Assab 73 E4
Aswan 53 J2
Aswan Dam 53 J1
Asyut 53 J2
Atbara 73 C5
Atbara, r. 11 F6, 73 D5
Atlas Mountains 11 C7, 52 D3
Axum 73 D4

Bamako 10 B6, 58 C3
Bambari 68 C4
Bandiagara Plateau 59 D3
Bandundu 68 B3
Bangui 11 D5, 68 C4
Bangweulu, Lake 81 B4
Banjul 10 A6, 58 A3
Bata 68 A4
Batu, mt. 73 D3
Bawiti 53 I2
Baydhabo 73 E2
Bazaruto Island 81 D2
Beaufort West 87 C1
Bechar 52 D3
Beida 53 H3
Beira 81 C3
Benghazi 53 H3

Benguela 68 B1
Béni Abbès 52 D3
Benin, Bight of 59 E2
Benin City 59 F2
Benoni 87 D2
Benue, r. 11 C5, 59 F2
Berbera 73 F4
Berberati 68 B4
Bethlehem 87 D2
Bié Plateau 11 D3, 68 B2
Bioko, i. 11 C5, 68 A4
Bissau 10 A6, 58 A3
Bizerte 53 F4
Black Volta, r. 59 D2
Blantyre 81 D3
Bloemfontein 87 D2
Bloemhof Dam 87 D2
Blue Nile, r. 11 F6, 73 C4
Bo 58 B2
Boa Vista, i. 58 I7
Bobo Dioulasso 59 D3
Bodélé Depression 11 B8, 68 B6
Bondo 68 C4
Bouaké 59 C2
Bouar 68 B4
Bouârfa 52 D3
Brava, i. 58 I7
Brazzaville 11 D4, 68 B3
Buchanan 58 C2
Bui Dam 59 D2
Bujumbura 11 E4, 77 A3
Bukavu 68 D3
Bukoba 77 B3
Bulawayo 81 B2
Bumba 68 C4
Burco 73 F3
Buta 68 D4
Butare 77 A3

Cabinda 11 D4, 68 B3
Cabora Bassa Dam 81 C3
Cairo 11 F8, 53 J3
Caledon, r. 87 D1
Cameroon, Mount 11 C5, 59 F1
Canary Islands 10 A7, 52 B2
Cape Town 87 B1
Casablanca 52 C3
Catherine, Mount 53 J2
Ceuta 52 D3
Chad, Lake 11 D6, 59 G3, 68 B6
Chari, r. 11 D6, 68 B5
Chilwa, Lake 81 D3
Chinde 81 D3
Chipata 81 C4
Choke Mountains 73 D4
Comoe, r. 59 D2
Conakry 10 A6, 58 B2
Congo, r. 11 D4, 11 E5, 68 B3, 68 C4
Congo Basin 11 D4
Constantine 52 F4
Cotonou 59 E2
Cuando, r. 68 C1
Cuanza, r. 68 B2
Cubango, r. 11 D3, 68 B1
Cuito, r. 68 C1

Dahlak Archipelago, isls. 73 E5
Dakar 10 A6, 58 A3
Dakhla 52 B1
Daloa 59 C2
Danakil Depression 73 E4
Dar es Salaam 77 C2
Darfur 72 A4
Dawa, r. 73 E2
De Aar 87 C1
Debre Markos 73 D4
Dese 73 D4
Dire Dawa 73 E3
Djibouti 11 G6, 73 E4
Dodoma 11 F4, 77 C2
Douala 59 F1
Drakensberg, mts. 11 E1, 87 D1
Durban 87 E2

East London 87 D1
Edward, Lake 68 D3, 77 A3
El Aaiun 10 A7, 52 B2
Eldoret 77 C4
El Faiyum 53 J2
El Fasher 72 B4
El Giza 53 J2
El Kharga 53 J2
El Obeid 72 C4
Elgon, Mount 11 F5, 77 B4
Emi Koussi, mt. 11 D6, 68 C7
En Nahud 72 B4
Entebbe 77 B4
Enugu 59 F2
Er Roseires 73 C4
Ethiopian Highlands 11 F5, 73 D3
Etosha Pan 86 B4
Eyasi, Lake 77 C3

Faya-Largeau 68 C6
Fderik 58 B5
Fès 52 D3
Fogo, i. 58 I7
Fouta Djallon, mts. 10 A6, 58 B3
Franceville 68 B3
Francistown 87 D3
Freetown 10 A5, 58 B2
Fuerteventura, i. 52 B2

Gabes 53 F3
Gaborone 11 D2, 87 D3
Gambia, r. 10 A6, 58 B3
Gao 59 D4
Garissa 77 C3
Garoua 59 G2
Gedaref 73 D4
George 87 C1
George, Lake 77 B3
Ghanzi 87 C3
Gitega 77 A3
Gobabis 87 B3
Gomera, i. 52 B2
Gonder 73 D4
Good Hope, Cape of 11 D1, 87 B1
Gore 73 D3
Grahamstown 87 D1
Gran Canaria, i. 52 B2
Great Karoo, mts. 11 E1, 87 C1

Great Rift Valley 77 B4
Groot, r. 87 C1
Grootfontein 87 B4
Guardafui, Cape 11 H6
Guinea, Gulf of 11 B5, 59 E1
Gulu 77 B4
Guna, mt. 73 D4
Gweru 81 B3

Harare 11 F3, 81 C3
Harer 73 E3
Hargeysa 73 E3
Hierro, i. 52 A2
High Atlas, mts. 52 C3
Hobyo 73 F3
Hoggar, mts. 11 C7, 52 E1
Huambo 68 B1
Hwange 81 B3

Ibadan 59 E2
Ife 59 E2
Igbo-Ukwe 59 F2
Ilebo 68 C3
Ilorin 59 E2
Impfondo 68 B4
Inga Dam 68 B3
Inhambane 81 D2
Inyangani, mt. 81 C3
Iringa 77 C2
Isiro 68 D4
Ituri Forest 68 D4

Jima 73 D3
Jinja 77 B4
Johannesburg 87 D2
Jonglei Canal 11 F1, 73 C3
Jos *Plateau* 59 F3
Juba 73 C3
Juba, r. 11 G5, 73 E2

Kaap Plateau 87 C2
Kabompo, r. 80 A4
Kabwe 81 B4
Kadoma 81 B3
Kaduna 59 F3
Kafue, r. 81 B3
Kafue Dam 81 B3
Kainji Dam 59 E2
Kainji Reservoir 59 E3
Kalahari Desert 11 E2, 87 C3
Kalemie 68 D2
Kamina 68 D2
Kampala 11 F5, 77 B4
Kananga 68 C3
Kankan 58 C3
Kano 59 F3
Kanye 87 D3
Kaolack 58 A3
Karasburg 87 B2
Kariba, Lake 11 E3, 81 B3
Kariba Dam 81 B3
Karonga 81 C4
Kasai, r. 11 D4, 68 C2
Kasama 81 C4
Kassala 73 D5
Katsina 59 F3

Kayes 58 B3
Keetmanshoop 87 B2
Kenya, Mount 11 F5, 77 C3
Khartoum 11 F6, 73 C5
Khartoum North 73 C5
Kigali 11 E4, 77 B3
Kigoma 77 A3
Kikwit 68 C3
Kilimanjaro, Mount 11 F4, 77 C3
Kilosa 77 C2
Kilwa 77 C2
Kimberley 87 C2
Kindu 68 D3
Kinshasa 11 D4, 68 B3
Kisangani 68 D4
Kismaayo 73 E1
Kisumu 77 B3
Kitale 77 C4
Kivu, Lake 68 D3, 77 A3
Klerksdorp 87 D2
Kossoul Dam 59 C2
Kosti 73 C4
Krugersdorp 87 D2
Kumasi 59 D2
Kunduchi 77 C2
Kwango, r. 11 D4, 68 B2
Kyle Dam 81 C2
Kyoga, Lake 11 F5, 77 B4

Labe 58 B3
Lagos 59 E2
Lalibela 73 D4
Lambaréné 68 A3
Lamu 77 D3
Lanzarote, i. 52 B2
Léré 68 B5
Libreville 11 C5, 68 A4
Libyan Desert 11 E7, 53 I2
Libyan Plateau 53 I3
Lichinga 81 D4
Likasi 68 D2
Lilongwe 11 F3, 81 C4
Limpopo, r. 11 F2, 81 C2, 87 D3
Lindi 77 C2
Little Karoo, mts. 87 C1
Livingstone 81 B3
Lobamba 11 F2, 87 E2
Lobatse 87 D2
Lobito 68 B1
Logone, r. 68 B5
Lomami, r. 11 E4, 68 D3
Lomé 11 C5, 59 E2
Loubomo 68 B3
Lualaba, r. 11 E4, 68 D3
Luanda 11 D4, 68 B2
Luangwa, r. 81 C4
Luanshya 81 B4
Lubango 68 B1
Lubumbashi 68 D2
Lüderitz 86 B2
Lulua, r. 68 C2
Lundazi 81 C4
Lusaka 11 E3, 81 B3
Luuq 73 E2

Index

DATE DUE

5-21-09	

DEMCO, INC. 38-2931